D1458893

WELCOME HOME

WELCOME HOME

*True Stories of Soldiers
Returning from World War II*

BEN WICKS

BLOOMSBURY

First published in Great Britain 1991
Bloomsbury Publishing Limited, 2 Soho Square, London W1V 5DE

Copyright © 1991 by Ben Wicks

The moral right of the author has been asserted

PHOTO SOURCES

The Hulton-Deutsch Collection: pages 1 *top & bottom*, 2 *top*, 3 *top*,
4 *top & bottom*, 5 *bottom*, 7 *top & bottom*, 8 *top & bottom*, 9 *top*,
10 *top & bottom*, 11 *top & bottom*, 15 *top*

Popperfoto: pages 2 *bottom*, 9 *bottom*, 12 *top & bottom*,
13 *top, middle & bottom*, 14, 16 *top & bottom*

Topham: pages 3 *bottom*, 5 *top*

The Trustees of the Imperial War Museum, London:
pages 6 *top & bottom*, 15 *bottom*

A CIP catalogue record for this book
is available from the British Library

ISBN 0-7475-1035-0

10 9 8 7 6 5 4 3 2 1

Typeset by Rowland Phototypesetting Limited
Bury St Edmunds, Suffolk
Printed in Great Britain by
Butler and Tanner Limited, Frome and London

To my sisters, Doll and Nan

Contents

Acknowledgements

Each year that passes pushes back in time an event that changed the lives of millions of people. For those who lived through World War II, the memories remain fresh for the simple reason that if it had not been for the war the lives they lead today would have been radically different.

Fortunately, in preparing this book we were able to tap into this period through the use of the dying art of letter writing. In these days of telecommunications, this ancient form is fast becoming a lost means of documenting our lives.

Newspapers as far afield as the Victoria Times-Colonist *in British Columbia, Canada and the London* Sunday Express *in England and a number of major magazines publicised the fact that we were looking for stories from those who had lived to see the end of World War II.* Woman's Weekly *and* Woman's Realm *magazines were especially helpful.*

At the Government of Ontario offices in London, Rosalind Nathan gallantly waded her way through the answers and passed them on to our Toronto office. Sandra Tooze edited the copy as it was handed to her and travelled extensively to gather research and information.

Thanks are also due to my editors in London, Penny Phillips and Caroline Taggart, the Imperial War Museum, the Island Trust, Rosemary Dixon and the London History Workshop, the British Limbless Ex-Servicemen's Association and Kathleen Halpin, CBE, of that wonderful organisation, the Women's Royal Voluntary Service.

The letters written by Enid Innes-Ker (page 44), Mavis Drake (pages

Acknowledgements

13 and 131) and Dame Anna Bryans (page 26) and the anonymous letter from a POW (page 35) are held in the Department of Documents in the Imperial War Museum, and are reproduced by permission of the Trustees of the museum. The letter written by Norman Ellison (page 35) is reproduced by permission of Liverpool Libraries and Arts.

Once again my agents, Matie Molinaro in Canada and Carolyn Brunton in London, were never further away than a telephone or fax machine.

My wife Doreen, as always, gave support and encouragement. And last, but most important, hundreds of strangers took pens in hand and relived their past on paper. Without them this book would be but an empty cover.

Introduction

1945. The war was coming to an end. It was not only at the front that the prospect of peace was cause for celebration. Far in the rear, those who had waited patiently at home also had reason to sigh with relief. For the first time in British history, civilians had witnessed the sort of death and destruction that had previously been the lot of those in the front lines. Being left behind to keep the home fires burning had been no guarantee of safety and those who had faced the nightly bombing felt, quite rightly, that they had just as much right to throw themselves into the victory celebrations as those who had worn a uniform.

But as the last cheers of the victory parades faded, men and women by the thousands faced a new world. Many were able to adjust, but after years of separation from their homes and loved ones, some returning servicemen found themselves less welcome and the difficulties impossible to overcome. Husbands and wives had grown apart; children were faced with the difficulty of accepting a 'new' parent.

Men and women alike were offered work that no longer satisfied them. Officers accustomed to salutes discovered that the pavements they were forced to pound in order to find work were much harder than the parade grounds.

When I began to research this book, it was my intention to document the stories of those service personnel who returned to Britain at the end of the conflict in Europe. But in preparing the manuscript, I found I was faced more and more with the role of those who had stayed behind. Many of them were women. Told by a desperate government that they were needed in the factories, filling in for men who had been called away to war, women filled the vacant spots without hesitation. Yet when the men came home, these countless 'Rosie the Riveters' were pushed out of their wartime jobs and forced to accept the traditional 'Doris Day' role once more. A lot of this book is their story.

1

Out of the Wire Cage

*B*Y MARCH 1945, *the once invincible German army was falling back on its capital. The Russians had begun a new offensive in February and were already within forty miles of Berlin. This advance had been good news for the people of Britain – especially those whose loved ones were prisoners of war in Europe. These POWs would be the first to arrive back home in any large numbers.*

Unfortunately, some of those prisoners found themselves forced to accompany their German guards as they retreated. Jack Poolton, a Canadian who had been taken prisoner in the raid on Dieppe, had been in chains for almost two years. He had to join thousands of other prisoners being marched westwards to avoid the advancing Russian army:

We found ourselves so far west that we were in danger of running into the advancing Americans. We could see all kinds of aircraft overhead. Bombers and fighters from Britain, Russian and the Americans. I was down to below eighty pounds, from 130 pounds, see, we'd been marching for four months. We were sleeping in barnyards overnight . . . we were never undercover . . . this particular morning we staggered into this town of Ditfurd and the American planes had strafed the town that day and there were dead horses and dead oxen and God knows what lying around as well as people. The people were very hostile . . . they were trying to get at us and spitting at us and our German guards put us into this farmyard. We hadn't had any bread for about four days . . . I was with two South African brothers I'd befriended. And one brother was almost gone . . . In the evening I remember climbing and looking over this barnyard wall and this Serbian was walking down the road and he said to me in German, 'Americans, ten kilometres,' and he pointed down the road. I went back inside and told the others. Most of them were too far gone. So I asked this New Zealander to join me in making a dash for it . . . I'd already escaped three times and been caught so it was in me to get out . . . anyway the New Zealand chap said, 'I'm almost gone, I'd only hold you up . . .' He was dead in the morning. And the South African wouldn't leave his brother. So I stayed and the next morning at six o'clock one of the South Africans went out . . . everyone had dysentery and there was waste everywhere . . . you were walking in it, lying in it . . . anyway he went by the barnyard doors which were ajar, and with his pants down he looked through the doors and he saw a jeep. He came running into me, pulling up his pants, and he said, 'There's a jeep out there.' So I staggered out and there was a jeep with three American soldiers in it. There was an officer, a driver and a radio operator. I said to the officer, 'Can I shake your hand?' and said, 'Where are you from?' He said 'Ohio!' I say to this day that I've seen the angels. I saw them that day, three of them.

Eddie Noll had been a German prisoner since the D-Day landings. He, too, was forced on a long march across Europe. For the last nine months of the war he worked in a stone quarry:

It had taken nearly three months to reach my final camp from the day of capture. Although I did not know it at the time, our working camp was not far to the north of Colditz.

We left our camp under German guard escort on 14 April 1945, and began a trek westwards towards the American lines, joining up with other similar marches along the way, as the German guards did not relish being taken by the Russians. One couldn't blame them. We didn't fancy them either and they were on our side.

A Canadian Royal Air Force pilot, Kingsley Brown, was shot down and captured during a bombing attack on Bremen. He was a prisoner of war for three years:

We'd known for two or three days that the Russian front lines were getting closer and at night we could see the explosions and fires as they moved up towards us. The day before, at about one o'clock, the Germans just left the camp. They simply lined up and the guard down at the gate tossed the keys over the gate and away they went. At about 6.15 the next morning the first Russian armoured car drove up to the gate. We'd been up all night waiting for it. We were about five weeks with the Russians before we got home.

A United Press newspaper man, Ken Beatty, had been taken prisoner and he was able to get out before us and, once he got into some free territory, he sent a telegram to my wife to let her know that I was okay.

The heavy bombing of Germany continued as the Allied forces advanced. The Americans crossed the Rhine in early March as British troops circled to the north and crossed the river on their way to the Ruhr. The last of the V2 weapons fell on Kent, followed two days later by the last of the V1s. For the first time in years, the British people could take their eyes off the skies and concentrate on what was happening around them.

On 1 May, as their Berlin bunker trembled from the exploding Russian shells, Hitler and his new wife, Eva Braun, shook the hands of the assembled staff, made their way slowly to the Führer's suite and closed the door. After giving Eva Braun poison to swallow, Hitler placed a gun in his mouth and pulled the trigger.

Goebbels and Bormann contacted the Russians, now less than a mile away, with proposals for a settlement. The answer was not the one they had hoped for. The Russians demanded that all German troops in Berlin surrender, including those still holed up in the bunker.

On the evening of the same day, Goebbels took his own life and those of his wife and six children. Bormann made his way out of the bunker with two others and died in an attempt to penetrate the Russian lines. Hamburg radio warned listeners that they were about to make an important announcement. After what was deemed appropriate Wagnerian music and the slow movement of Bruckner's Seventh Symphony came the crash and roll of military drums. The voice of an announcer introduced the new Führer, Grand Admiral Dönitz. It was Dönitz's task to tell the German people that Hitler was dead; he then declared that they would fight on against the 'advancing Bolshevik enemy' and concluded with the words, 'God will not forsake us after so much suffering and sacrifice.'

But the end was near and Dönitz knew it. Anxious to surrender to the Western Allies rather than the Russians, he stalled to give the Germans time to move as many troops and refugees as possible away from the advancing Russians. Unfortunately for him Eisenhower was not prepared to delay the surrender, and threatened to close the entire front, preventing any German refugees from entering the Allied lines.

At 1.30 a.m. on 7 May Dönitz contacted his general, Jodl, from his new headquarters and instructed him to sign the unconditional surrender documents. It was 2.41 in the morning when the group of players made their way to a small red schoolhouse at Reims. General Bedell Smith signed for the Allies, with General Ivan Suslaparov as a witness for Russia and General François Sevez for France. Admiral Hans Georg von Friedeburg and General Alfred Jodl signed for Germany. Standing back from the table Jodl asked if he could say a few words. Bedell Smith nodded.

'With this signature,' he said, 'the German people and the German armed forces are, for better or worse, delivered into the hands of the victors . . . In this hour I can only hope that the victor will treat them with generosity.'

It was over. A strange silence crept across the continent. It had been five years and eight months since the start of the war on 3 September 1939. During that time millions of men and women had died. The veils of silence had been torn aside to reveal the horrors of the concentration camps. Many of Europe's cities were in ruins, but at long last the Thousand-Year Reich had been brought to a halt and, in the late spring of 1945, it ceased to exist.

2

Has It Finally Ended?

*P*EACE, WHEN IT *came, was a strange let-down. For years millions had dreamed of a world that would suddenly come alive with thousands of lights. The truth was that in May 1945 few knew when the war in Europe would finally be declared over. They had followed the progress of Montgomery's army as it crossed the Rhine and the successful linking of the American and Russian forces that cut Germany in two. For weeks Union Jacks had been on sale ready to wave in a frenzy of celebration.*

But even the news that Hitler had killed himself failed to produce the expected declaration of peace. On the following day, 2 May, the BBC interrupted programmes to report the surrender of all Germans in Italy. That same evening the fall of Berlin was announced. On 4 May all German troops in Denmark were reported to have surrendered. In fact, the first news of Germany's final unconditional surrender did not come from the government at all, but was picked up from a German radio broadcast at lunchtime on 7 May.

Joyce Hampson remembers that speculation went on for days:

The war in Europe seemed to trickle to an end somehow. I remember than on the previous Friday I was on night shift. Sometime after midnight a rumour flew around the factory that the war was over. It had been on the twelve o'clock news. We were in a group discussing this bit of information when the works superintendent came by and he told us nothing had been confirmed and if anything important came through we would be told, so we carried on working. Nothing definite had come through by Monday. Still, lots of speculation was going on. Then either that night or Tuesday, as I walked home after the day's work, when I and some of my workmates reached the main road outside the factory, we noticed that someone had a flag flying from the bedroom window. When we walked over the canal bridge, another flag was flying. Is the war over and they haven't told us? we wondered. 'Well,' I said, 'when we get to the top of my street if my mam has got one out we will know it's over.' Mam had got two out.

That night we listened to Churchill telling us, 'Well done,' and that we could now have a day off from our labours and then back with a will to finish the Japs off. We were all busy finding anything that would do for red, white and blue bunting to adorn the street. Photos of Winnie and the Royal Family were stuck in windows and on walls. The atmosphere was terrific. There was a collection for contributions of food to give the kids a party the next day. VE Day. The Richards family brought their piano out into the street and Johnnie Richards, who was about fourteen then, played his accordion. A bonfire was lit on the bomb crater, the site of eight houses that had been bombed in the November blitz. We were dancing in the street and singing all the wartime songs, going round the area to visit the other street parties that were going on. Heaven knows what time it was before we all packed up.

Our postwoman had gone to work on VE Day because, as she told me, there were letters for young women whose menfolk were overseas and a letter from them would help to make their day. I, for one, was one of the recipients of a letter that day and was I thankful. My husband had been on leave in April and I had not received any news from him since then. In the letter he said there were rumours going round that the war was finished.

After those few days everyone settled down to the routine once more. The only difference was that now we had no blackout and the streetlights were lit – well, what was left of them – and we knew that we were safe from air-raids.

The war in the Far East ended very suddenly, as history tells. We went mad again. This time I went to the city centre and we were all doing the conga around Broadgate. It was a terrific time to have lived through. In the meantime I had obtained a house of my own to live in. My husband, Tom, was demobbed in October 1946 and he went back to work for his old employer and settled down to Civvy Street well, with no hang-ups. He kept in touch with a few of his old army mates, but vowed never to join even a Christmas club after that lot.

Before an official announcement was made, flags were fluttering throughout the nation. Tradesmen, wary of the street celebrations to come, wisely began to shutter the windows of their shops to protect them from the anticipated crowds.

People gathered outside Buckingham Palace shouting, 'We want the King!' Convinced that VE Day was about to be declared, they just needed a signal to begin the celebrations. Meanwhile, the BBC were anxiously waiting for the government to give them permission to broadcast the news.

One woman waiting for a train at Euston remembers the crowd suddenly falling silent as these words came over the loudspeaker: 'Here is an important announcement . . . ' When the official went on to inform them that the 4.09 for Northampton was leaving from platform seven and not platform four as shown on the indicator, there was a large roar of indignation from the disappointed crowd.

Crowds outside the House of Commons and the Mansion House slowly made their way home after being told that the long-awaited Churchill broadcast would not be given that evening. The Prime Minister's official announcement would be on the radio the next day at three o'clock, in accordance with arrangements made with Russia and the US.

The most exciting item in the evening news was from the Board of Trade, anxious to 'do their bit' to encourage a celebration: 'Until the end of May you may buy cotton bunting without coupons, as long as it is red, white or blue and does not cost more than one and threepence a square yard.'

As the light faded on a remarkable day the first flickers of bonfires began to splutter against the night sky. Soldiers, sailors and airmen linked arms with their girls and, with paper hats tipped at jaunty angles, made their way laughing and singing through the streets of London, which by now were festooned with bobbing balloons and the crackle of twirling rattles.

During the night a tremendous thunderstorm poured torrential rain on streets that would soon be covered with dancing feet.

The patient population woke on the morning of Tuesday, 8 May to the sounds of their radios blasting out victory music played on a cinema organ. At 3 p.m. the Prime Minister finally sat down in a room at Number 10 Downing Street and declared that the representatives of the German High Command had signed the act of unconditional surrender in Europe.

'The German war is therefore at an end . . . Long live the cause of freedom. God save the King.'

After his public broadcast Churchill made his way to the House of Commons. The car carrying him was helped along by thousands who circled it, pushing and shoving, anxious to shake the hand of the man who had led them to victory. From the House of Commons he headed for the church of St Martin's in the Field to give thanks.

With his familiar lisping delivery he read the words of the 124th psalm: 'Even as a bird out of the fowler's net escapes away, so is our soul set free.' From the church he was taken to a balcony overlooking St James Park. Waving his arms and repeatedly giving his world-renowned 'V' sign, he was, it seemed to his bodyguard, obviously relishing every moment, 'like a schoolboy on an outing'.

Not everyone learned the news via the radio. Jean Hewitt heard about the war ending as she was walking home, not thinking of anything in particular:

A woman ran out from her house shouting, 'It's over, it's over!' I just stood still while tears gushed from my eyes and I stood sobbing for ages before continuing home with an odd flat feeling that life as I knew it for the past five years was going to change drastically.

But I was soon swept up with everyone else on the exciting high of the war being over. My sister suggested that we go up to the West End for the evening and never since then have I been a part of such a relieved and happy multitude. Nobody was doing anything out-rageous, just wandering about. Everybody was laughing and talk-ing to each other. Good will and good humour flowed everywhere. The relief from our fears and trials and the rosy future facing us were totally overwhelming.

Every street organised parties. Everyone pitched in to help provide cakes, sandwiches and jellies. Trestle tables were found and set up down the middle of the street. Bunting was raked out and strung from window across to opposite window and Union Jacks fluttered from every conceivable spot. Somebody brought a piano out on to the pavement. All the kids had their bun fight in the afternoon and the adults continued to 'knees up', drink and sing and release their bottled-up fears long into the night. It was quite amazing how all the goodies for the party materialised. I suppose people thought there was no further need to hang on to their meagre hoardings and were glad to share with everyone else. It was a magical day.

Later on, when the official victory parade was arranged, I went to town again but it wasn't the same. The whole atmosphere was different. The spontaneity was missing. The pushing and snarling at each other to get a better view lacked the wonderful comradeship of my previous visit to town on the day that the peace was declared.

The Women's Voluntary Service were out in force, as they had been throughout the war. Kathleen Halpin was the regional administrator for the Greater London Region and had made her way to Buckingham Palace:

One of my most vivid memories of V E Day was seeing a young girl, who must have been about thirty-two. This girl had been our clothing organiser for the London Region until she was called up at the age of thirty, and she chose the police. On V E Day I was in front of Buckingham Palace and I suddenly looked up and saw a police officer standing on a pedestal (because she was a rather short person) directing the traffic the other way round the Victoria Memorial. Because of the crowds of people, the police were told to make everyone go the other way round. Now the regular policeman had gone off at ten o'clock for a break. There was a lull between the people who'd come early and those who were to come later when the lights were all on and royalty would be on the balcony looking down. So, there was a lull before the next duty of policemen and they'd left this young girl standing on the pedestal, with quite a good crowd still there, making everyone go the opposite way to what they were used to.

When the lights were turned on it was so brilliant to see it. There were so many things that one had almost forgotten.

As the light began to fade on that happy day Harold Nicolson MP found himself walking through a jolly crowd in Trafalgar Square and wrote in his diary:

The National Gallery was alive with every stone outlined in floodlighting, and down there was Big Ben with a grin upon his illuminated face. The statue of Nelson was picked out by a search-light, and there was the smell of distant bonfires in the air. I walked to the Temple and beyond. Looking down Fleet Street one saw the best sight of all – the dome of St Paul's rather dim-lit, and then above it a concentration of searchlights upon the huge golden cross. So I went to bed.

That was my victory day.[1]

Searchlights crisscrossed the sky and added to the party spirit that now threaded its way through the streets of London. Not all searchlight operators stayed at their post, though. Helena Payne was in the ATS on a searchlight unit and was unable to resist joining the party:

On VE Day everybody was absolutely full of joy and they wanted the searchlight girls to swing the searchlights around the sky. On VE Day when we knew all the crowds were coming up to London, three or four of us decided we would go AWOL because we didn't want to stay on the searchlights swinging them around the sky while everyone was up here in London having a booming good time, you see. So we went AWOL and the other girls were a little bit chicken; they decided they had better stay at their post.

We had a wonderful time with all these people we met when we went AWOL. I lost my handbag in the crowd, but somebody found it and got in touch with me and gave it back, which I thought was very nice. We went back to our site the next day and, of course, we all got put on a charge and came in front of the officer and said that we had wanted to get in amongst all the people having a good time. I think all we got was a few extra chores. That didn't go down well with the other girls because they could have done the same thing.

[1] From Harold Nicolson: *Diaries and Letters 1939–45*, edited by Nigel Nicolson (Collins, 1967).

Doreen Barnley still has a clear memory of her feelings on VE Day:

'Glad' – what an understatement. Forgotten how we felt? Never, not if I lived a thousand years. In London, after the deprivations, danger and heartache, we went crazy. The weather was in tune with the celebrations. We had the day off work. My friend Eileen Meekey and I went to the West End. The people were in the thousands, everyone singing, dancing, kissing. We moved with the crowds down the Mall to Buckingham Palace. 'We want George! We want Elizabeth!' was rewarded with Their Majesties' balcony appearances. The crowd was so dense anyone fainting was lifted horizontal above the crowds and carried off to cheers.

We spent all day enjoying ourselves. Come evening there was no transport, so we made our way home to N19 by foot through streets where the remains of bonfires were still glowing, no doubt fuelled with those ugly blackout blinds. We had eaten only a snack all day. When we found an all-night tea stall at Tufnell Park, we sat in the gutter and wolfed a stale roll – it was nectar – to help us on our way. We arrived home at two in the morning and, to my mother's inquiry, 'Did you enjoy yourselves?' the answer was, 'Oh, Mum, I'm so tired but it was wonderful, wonderful.'

Anne Taylor remembers VE Day with a laugh. It was rather ironic:

Actually, I was ill on VE Day and couldn't go out. Funny, wasn't it? Staying on the Isle of Dogs all through the war and then when there was a bit of merriment, I was in bed.

Mixed in the crowds that flocked to London that day was a twenty-four-year-old intelligence officer from Canada, Pierre Berton. Like most servicemen stationed close enough to the city, he and his friends had made their way to London to join in the festivities:

We went to the Canadian Legion offices where they were having a big celebration. I knew it well since I had a room there. I had been there a couple of months before and taken out a certain girl who worked there. At that time she and I had shared a bottle of rye.

Anyway, I found her again on VE Day in the middle of this celebration and said, 'Let's go out and have a drink.'

The place was jammed. I mean everybody was going crazy. The streets were full of people cheering and the pubs had broken out all the scotch that they'd been claiming that they didn't have, but in truth, they'd been saving it.

So we pushed into one of the bars and I said, 'I'll get you a scotch.' She said, 'You'd better make it a double.' So I brought back the drinks and she gulped hers down, then turned to me and said, 'Drink your scotch, drink it all.' I said, 'What the hell for? I want to take my time. Anyway, why are you forcing me to drink so fast?'

She replied, 'Well, this is the first time I've ever had to tell a man that he's about to become a father.' I said, 'Oh God, well let's do something about it.' She said, 'No, no, no! I want you to leave. You didn't seduce me, I seduced you. I had my eyes wide open. Anyway, I've got a guy who wants to marry me and I don't want any complications. So I don't want to hear from you again. Goodbye!'

So I left . . . And that was my VE Day.

The London Daily Mirror *celebrated in its own way by allowing the star of its popular strip cartoon, Jane, to appear without clothes. Others found a more traditional way of giving thanks and made their way by the thousands to St Paul's Cathedral.*

Doris McCartney was living with her parents on the Isle of Dogs in London when she heard church bells ringing:

People were all coming out of their houses, putting on their coats, and they had a service straight away. The next day was a national holiday and there were some spontaneous parties, but most of the children had parties later, on the weekend, when they had time to get organised. They were all street parties.

Most of the servicemen when they came home they'd got banners saying 'Welcome Home' across the road or outside their house and they had family parties. They went on quite a long while, some of them. Until that time we hadn't been able to get out very much, especially on the island, which was so heavily bombed all the way through. It was a great relief to everybody. You got started sorting yourself out again, taking all the blackout off the windows. Gradually things came back. You could get crockery with fancy work on it. It had all been utility grade during the war and things were hard to get. Gradually things got easier.

Outside London, local dignitaries took centre stage. From village hall to city hall balcony the victory message was delivered to the celebrating crowds. Mavis Young (now Drake) was in the Women's Land Army based in Lincolnshire. On 8 May they were given the day off:

I was returning to the farm on Dick's, the horse's, back as dusk was falling when the farmer shouted to me that the war was over, and he was going back to the village pub to celebrate. I thought he was joking, but when I arrived back at the rectory and the excited chatter of the other girls, I was convinced it was true, and we spent the evening crowded around the radio to catch every crumb of news. We went wild! Grabbing our bikes we raced through the lanes and villages, whooping, singing and shouting and calling out to everybody we saw. Passing the gates of an aerodrome, we stopped to talk to four air force boys, who invited us to their mess to celebrate. Now, apart from the odd sherry at Christmas, I had never touched alcohol, but allowed myself to be persuaded that cider wouldn't do me any harm! Oh dear, how wrong they were. I have a hazy recollection of the four of us, and our bikes, being driven back to the rectory in some sort of truck, but more than that has disappeared into oblivion.

At about eleven o'clock that evening, the Princesses Elizabeth and Margaret, escorted by two plainclothes officers, joined the throngs near the palace. King George wrote in his diary, 'Poor dears, they have never had any fun yet.'

This was true for many children who were unaware of what it was like to live in peacetime. Seeing the main buildings of London flooded with lights was an awesome experience for those who had grown up in the blackout. Valerie Tomblin-Booth was approaching her ninth birthday and, like the princesses, saw the end of the war with a child's eyes:

As you will note by my age, I had no real idea of life without war. My limited span had been governed by war: rationing, raids, fear, the lack of males unless in uniform, female teachers, mostly old and rescued from retirement, air-raid shelters with their own peculiar damp, musky smell, the acrid smell of smoke following a bombing. To all of my generation this was the only life we knew, so, therefore, accepted. At the age of nine I had never seen a streetlamp working or a shop window lit up. Buses crawled in semi-darkness, their headlamps covered with gauze, revealing just a cross of light. Likewise, the windows were blotted out with a fine mesh.

None of us then could envisage quite what would happen when the war was over and each had hopes and dreams. Some envisaged shops so full of sweets they would never sell out.

Others dreamed of ice-cream (something few could recall and only heard described by our elders) piled high in dishes. My personal dream was to acquire my own German!

I went to school as usual. We had assembly, prayed for the King, the serving soldiers, etc., and disbanded to class only to be recalled later. The headmistress had a very important message – be quiet or she wouldn't tell us. We shuffled and waited: 'Children, the war is over. We have won. Now let us pray.' These words will be with me until I die. The hall full of usually fidgeting children was utterly silent. None of us really knew what this meant, what to expect, what the future would hold or what difference it would make to our lives.

Having prayed, we then heard the magic words, 'You may have the rest of today off.' We broke ranks and ran. No more gas-masks strapped to our backs, no more sirens, no more raids. I ran, skipped and hopped to my grandmother's (my mother, a widow, was doing war work). I danced up the garden, 'Gran, Gran, it's over.' Into the house I dashed. She sat there, tears flowing, but not of happiness. Her youngest son was killed at Dunkirk. He was twenty-one. The end of the war brought the realisation he would never come home.

I anticipated a hasty tea and going to join my mates in the street, to be part of all the excitement. This was not to be. My grandmother said, 'I have something I've been saving for you, for this very day.' This was added excitement until I saw her carefully unwrap a piece of wide red, white and blue ribbon, which she proceeded to tie in a massive, floppy bow in my hair! I felt an idiot but intended removing it once I escaped to talk with my friends about where I'd obtain my German.

My grandmother's next blow to my euphoria was to pick flowers and announce we would be going to the cemetery, which we did. How I envied those in the street as I trudged to the cemetery.

Two weeks later, with a committee organised, the party was arranged – a huge affair (by my standards) with everyone contributing what they could foodwise. An ancient set of coloured lights was draped from tree to tree. There was a piano and the biggest bonfire I'd ever seen. The party was under way.

In our small area there were many at war, missing, dead and one young lad's parents had had no knowledge of him for months. His mother contributed and did her best for everyone, disguising her own sadness. But her efforts were with one stipulation: a chair was to be placed at the table for her son.

This wish was complied with, but it left an air of sadness with the empty chair. When we had eaten as much as we could, the fire was lit and the pianist played. In the midst of this jolly atmosphere the mother with the missing son suddenly let out a scream and promptly collapsed . . . We all looked in her direction and, like something from a film, her son was coming up the road, knapsack on his back! The party was complete, as was her joy. Only my grandmother retired indoors.

I went to bed tired, happy and extremely full. The party went on all night, with only a filthy street and smouldering ashes to show in the morning. The party proved the war was over.

Some time later, there was a massive celebration in London. My mother was determined I would see this grand parade of troops and royalty . . . and with this in mind, we left Watford just after 6 a.m. for London. The crowds were enormous. It seemed odd finding London so noisy as we made our way to a vantage point in a small side road. Although with good intention, it was not a good position, especially for me. Being small, I went to the front. The barriers were up. I stood behind a very large policeman.

The wait seemed endless until I heard music, bands and noise. I glanced around to tell my mother it was coming. She had gone, lost in the welter of people!

I panicked and started crying. Eventually someone noticed, but this coincided with the cars carrying Churchill, Montgomery and others I failed to recognise through my tears.

My hysteria mounted until the policeman and a soldier lifted me high in the air. My mother, now pushed to the back, called my name at the moment the King, Queen and two princesses drew level. I had a wonderful view of the entire Royal Family, but it was lost on me at that moment as my panic was ultimate. A solution was found as there was no way through the crush of people. I was passed over the heads of the crowd until reaching my mother, whose panic matched my own, thinking she had lost me.

After such a trauma, I wanted to go home, but we stayed in town until evening, saw the Royal Family on the palace balcony, then left the crowds dancing in the Mall. Watford seemed a haven after such a traumatic, tiring day but, in reflection, it was possibly the trauma that makes the event still so vivid in my mind at fifty-four years of age!

I have a legacy of war – I loathe crowds, being in confined spaces and living in the flight path of military jets. I have been known to 'scramble' eggs in my hands when the planes fly low.

For many, the celebrations were marred by the knowledge that loved ones were never coming home.

Bette Gittings had two brothers serving overseas:

One came back, one did not. I remember standing amid a crowd of hooting, shouting people but I just stood there, remembering all that my family had been through and was still going through. At twenty-two years of age I wondered when I would feel free to hoot and holler too, when I would truly feel that the war was over for my mother.

To this day I am haunted by the short memory of my younger brother and the too-short years that we had together as a family. When the telegram came my mother handed it to me. I knew then what was meant by utter disbelief. 'Missing in action', but my mother lived on hope, month after month and year after year. At regular intervals she received messages from the government. After a six-month period my brother was declared legally dead. My mother received his personal belongings, except his Rolls razor, and this gave her some weird hope that he wasn't dead but just away somewhere and that he had taken his razor with him. Slim straws indeed to grasp, but she hung on tight.

More papers came, from every air force officer one could imagine and from assorted government officials, until one day she broke down with an agonising cry, 'Why won't they leave me alone?' She wrote to the mothers of the other crew members. She wanted to be in touch, she needed that link. Hopefully someone knew something that she did not.

'Missing in action' gives a smidgen of hope, often never fulfilled. Death is so final and to have used that word would have been kinder in the long run. Mothers such as mine are the unsung heroes. They could do nothing but wait, wait and wait.

Marcia Vardon was teaching in a Plymouth junior school, and had to explain to the children that the war in Europe was finally over:

The headmistress, knowing I was a Methodist local preacher, asked me to speak to the children, reminding them that there was still fighting going on in the Far East, and that some of their fathers would not be home for some time yet. Many stories came to light through the innocent honesty of the children:

'Mummy's having a new baby soon; Daddy's not very pleased though, because he's been away for three years — I don't know why he's cross about it.'

'We've got a new baby, a special one, he's black — all the others are white.'

For Terry Godwin the end of the war was no surprise. His mother had told him some weeks before that the Russians were in Berlin and that any day now peace would be declared. Many houses displayed Union Jacks, though some were flying the Russian 'hammer and sickle'. But for Terry there was only one flag:

Union Jack flags were flown from people's windows, including our own. The flag was dug out from the loft. Monty, our dog, was given a bow of red, white and blue ribbon. If proof was really needed as to how important and dramatic the news was, it was supplied when a man who lived in our road gave me sixpence when he saw me in the street that day. He was widely known for his meanness and had never been known to give anyone anything. A 1945 Scrooge, in effect, and he had given me sixpence!

Jim Giles wondered what a peacetime Britain would be like:

Would there be bluebirds flying over the white cliffs of Dover the way Vera Lynn told us in song? Would we now be able to switch on the lights at home without drawing the blackout curtains? As a boy nearing his sixteenth birthday, my thoughts were on sweet rationing – would it end soon so that I could celebrate with chocolate? But then it would be nice to have Dad home again – he was a London fireman and saw a lot of the local action. Mum would be relieved, too – air-raids terrified her. Victory over Europe Day, or VE Day, turned out to be a great day of celebration with many street parties. What's more, the weather was absolutely perfect.

I got hold of some red, white and blue crêpe paper and strung this through the spokes of my bicycle. My pals copied the idea, after which we cycled round and round our district feeling very jolly and patriotic. Some of the other boys collected some old musical intruments: a bugle, a kettle-drum, a harmonica and a bicycle pump made into a sort of whistle. They marched up our main road and into the High Street, attempting to create some form of music. It was all good, harmless fun. People laughed – real laughter – culminating in the released tension of the long, dark, war years. What a great day it was. Although I was a mere lad at the time, I could still, nevertheless, feel the wonderful atmosphere that seemed to hang over London. It was a happy day for Britain.

The morning VE Day was declared, Brian Payton was in a barn in Margaret Roding in Essex, with his school's harvest camp, 'digging for victory':

Heaven knows what we were harvesting in May! For reasons I cannot tell I had always been impressed by old reports of the celebrations in London on Mafeking Night and I thought, I sure as hell am not going to miss this one.

Our assistant headmaster, who was in charge of us boys, had

informed us of the news at breakfast and said that after supper we would all have a bonfire and sit around for a singsong. The idea of choruses of *Green Grow the Rushes Oh* and *Hearts of Oak*, etc., to say nothing of being allowed to stay up until 10.30, didn't have much appeal to me. So, as we boys left our campsite to cycle off to the farms where we were working, when they all turned left I turned right and headed back towards London.

I set off into central London later in the afternoon to merge with the thousands that had gathered in Piccadilly Circus and outside the palace. I have memories of hundreds of people dancing and singing and of two drunken American sailors up a lamppost in Piccadilly, trying to rock it out of the ground, whilst two US 'snowballs' patiently waited at the base for their descent. I distinctly remember sitting on the railings that surrounded the descent to a public toilet in Piccadilly, whilst trying to preserve my innocence from some older person of the same sex, finding retreat the only escape.

Exhausted by about three o'clock in the morning, I sought somewhere to sit down until the buses started running again. I miraculously found a space on a bench in St James's Park, only to find myself again defending my virtue from some airman! All in all, a night to remember!

The real fun started the next day. At suppertime we were all assembled at our tables ready to eat. After grace our assistant headmaster said something like this:

'I wish to draw your attention to the fact that we have here amongst us someone who thinks he can do as he likes, has no sense of responsibility and deems it quite appropriate to wander off to London and spend the night leaning on a lamppost and whistling at girls.

'This is the sort of boy who causes wars! I would suggest to you that he be treated as he deserves and be sent to Coventry!'

Following this suggestion, all those sitting near me slid along their benches, leaving me alone. To give them credit, though, after supper they all wanted much more detailed accounts than our master had wanted of what it had been like. 'Leaning on lampposts whistling at girls!' Nothing could have been farther from the truth. Now, if he had been talking about V J Day, well, that's a different story.

Ann Nind had been evacuated to Satterthwaite, in the Lake District, during the war. Her father brought her back to London for VE night. She found the atmosphere incredible:

London was one large party; servicemen and women and adults of all ages thronged and sang and danced. We saw Churchill come out on the balcony by the Cenotaph and wave and give the V sign. The crowd went wild. We walked in St James's Park and there were fountains of dancing water with changing coloured lights in the lakes. It was beautiful, fascinating, miraculous and unforgettable.

I would like to point out how many changes and adjustments children of that era had to make, and made successfully, but I found the change back to city life by far the most difficult. City children, certainly those in middle-class girls' schools, did not have the same qualities of open and accepting friendship present in the children of Satterthwaite.

I had a North Country accent and phraseology, and I was behind in my schoolwork. I hated that so-called 'good' school. The next four years were lonely, an unmitigated hell of an experience, and the education was fraudulent.

Nell Brown was fifteen when the war ended and lived in Bexleyheath, Kent:

It was a glorious time. We all went to London to a big street party. Had a good knees-up – a wonderful time.

You could tell the men who had been demobbed by the suits they wore. I remember the soldiers stationed in Woolwich used to fight a lot. When they saw the redcoats coming they used to run. There was still a lot of heartache after the war: people knowing their loved ones weren't coming back, people still mourning the people they lost in the Blitz and the homes they had lost, and then the horror of finding out about Belsen and the other prisoner-of-war camps. When you went to the pictures you would see it on the news. It made people sick and you could hear them crying over it.

The end of the war meant to me sleeping safely in your own bed and having the satisfaction of knowing that bloody old Hitler was dead.

Many of the revellers on VE Night had been drinking but were not unduly rowdy. In the streets men and women in the uniforms of the Allied nations linked arms and danced their way through the crowds. Women from ATS, WAAF and the land army joined factory workers, filled with a new feeling of their value and independence.

Some servicemen, like Ted Radford in the Royal Canadian Air Force, found the need to be alone:

I was a flight engineer on Lancasters and Halifaxes at 6 Group, RCAF Bomber Command, 427 Squadron, Leeming, Yorkshire. I had just completed a tour of operations in April 1945 and our crew was then given two weeks' leave. As usual on leaves, I had my travel permit made out to Land's End. I seldom got beyond London unless I felt like visiting my relatives in Devon.

While in London I bumped into some buddies from the 427. 'Hey, Radford,' they said, 'the rest of your crew was recalled and they have flown a Lanc back to Canada without you.'

I was deeply disturbed so I went AWOL for three weeks and returned to 427 around 6 May 1945. I was put on a charge and appeared before the adjutant. He was lenient and said he wanted to keep an eye on me, but there was no room for me on the Leeming base, so he shipped me out to the satellite base (Croft, I think).

Well, I ended up there on the morning of 8 May. Of course I was the last of their interests that day! Someone said, 'You are assigned to Nissen Hut Number 3.' I went there in the afternoon and, to my shock and surprise, I found the hut filled with the usual number of bunk beds, but all were bare of bedding and no one else lived in this hut but me.

I lay on my bunk as dark approached with an excellent view of the main hangar as they rolled out the barrels and began celebrating. I was so despondent and angry I refused myself the pleasure of joining the celebration. By 9 p.m. I grimly rolled over in my bed and went to sleep. Fortunately, they and their celebrations were far enough away that they could not disturb my sleep and I awoke in the morning well rested.

Shortly afterwards, they told me I had been held back when my crew left because they wanted me to be an instructor. I politely told them to shove it.

For those serving overseas, the news of peace seemed to elicit a more subdued reaction. Ed Bruce, a soldier serving in Holland, remembers:

All we got was a pint of beer, nothing else.

Bill Dyer, a sailor in the Mediterranean, says:

We didn't celebrate anything.

John Frost served in the Eleventh Armoured Division. The following is part of the letter he wrote home to his mother on VE Day:

Dear Mum,

It's VE Day, fighting has ceased. It finds Stan and I safe and well – we have much to be thankful for. Our celebrations will come when we walk up the garden path – I think it will come before Christmas for both of us.

This afternoon we all listened to Churchill broadcast over the radio – it put the official touch to things that it was all over. It's now eight o'clock; at nine we shall be hearing a speech from the King.

From the radio news we have all learnt of the wild celebrations going on in London and other cities. Wish I could see all the flags flying and hear the bells pealing – the ringing sounds nice over the wireless . . .

This morning on first parade we had three special orders of the day read out to us. They were congratulatory messages from army commanders on our achievements in Germany. One from General Dempsey was addressed to this division only and he congratulated the Eleventh Armoured on their recent capture of Lubeck and the advance to the Baltic Sea . . .

The weather today has been glorious. I'm getting quite tanned – this may be due to the fact that every time I drive my vehicle I keep my windows open. The crossing of the great River Elbe was by pontoon bridge – it was very bumpy but I managed to get across safely, though I must admit feeling hot under the collar.

I have now driven over 1,200 miles from Normandy to northern Germany.

The other day I had the pleasure of driving a jeep to Hamburg – people were actually waving to us. We must not reply.

Along the road today have passed thousands more German soldiers and airmen. They drive their own vehicles, they look battle-worn and completely tired. They prefer to give themselves up to us than to the Russians.

Also on the roads making their own way from the Russians are hundreds of German civilians. Those that have horses and carts have household belongings piled up on the carts – many are walking, women and children too. VE Day is very different in Germany.

There is not much victory to be seen here in the army – today we have been holding the usual parades and working as usual. We still carry our rifles loaded everywhere we go – you can't trust every German to surrender quietly.

This is our third week without bread – it's biscuits and bully beef, not forgetting good old tinned sardines, pilchards and powdered potatoes. There is no beer for the boys – so VE Day is just another day out . . . In a few moments the King will speak – the hut here is crowded. There are several German beds in here for it was formerly a German soldiers' billet. The radio is German too – the reception is excellent. Some of the boys are in bed writing letters, others are sitting up and all ears are open. The anthem has just played – the major is present . . . the speech is over. The King has certainly improved his manner of speaking. The news is now on – I'm sure you too are listening.

And so, Mum, I come to a close – what the future will be not many people know but let's pray that this is the last war in Europe. They say demobilisation will take place six weeks from now, so roll on No. 27 and let's get out – right out.

Cheerio Mum.

Hope you are well, also Les, Doll and Audrey.

All my love from your loving son,

John xxxxxxx

Perhaps the most raucous and explosive responses to the news of the end of the war in Europe occurred in Halifax, Nova Scotia. Jake Isbister was serving there on board the destroyer H M C S Restigouche:

Our task was to escort troop ships off the eastern coast of Canada. We were in Halifax when the war ended. As I recall it was 10 a.m. when it was declared the war was all over. Needless to say pandemonium broke loose. We were all expecting this in the last few days but when it was made official, let me tell you, the lid literally blew off the city of Halifax.

We had several civilian dock workers aboard doing minor repairs. They just dropped their tools and ran ashore. Can you imagine every ship in harbour blowing its whistle? Bear in mind that Halifax was the main eastern staging point in Canada for all North Atlantic convoys. Safe to say, ships numbered in the hundreds: merchant marine and naval. Also, bear in mind that Halifax had the greatest concentration of troops – navy, army and air force – anywhere in Canada. Put this all together and you have the makings of a celebration to end all celebrations. All those long, weary years of separation from home and family, those perilous weeks at sea constantly battling the enemy and our real enemy, the cruel sea, were over. We would be going home.

I fully realise it is easy for me to say this now, but the whole thing was very badly handled. As I stated earlier, we all knew the end was very near and I am, to this day, very critical of the authorities – armed forces and government – for not anticipating the trouble when the end came. They should at least have tried to organise celebrations in local parks, parade squares or military establishments. Absolutely nothing was planned. Instead, what happened was that everything promptly closed. You couldn't even buy a soft drink.

The trouble all started at the local brewery. Crowds gathered outside the gates, then closed, demanding beer. Civilians had joined in the milling crowds. It was inevitable that they stormed the gate and went over the fence and took the beer. All of it! The brewery was cleaned out in very short order. It was not long after that, fortified by the beer, the liquor stores were next. By then things were completely out of control. A streetcar was commandeered, turned on its side and set fire to. The fire department arrived and attempted to extinguish the fire. The fire axes were then taken and the hoses cut.

The stores along Barrington Street came under attack. Plate glass windows were shattered and looting was the order of the day. We were getting reports throughout the day about the rioting. Later on in the day I went ashore and, believe me, it was a sight I shall never forget. As I walked up the street, people were coming towards me with their arms laden with bottles of liquor. I asked a civilian policeman where they were getting all the liquor. His reply: 'From the liquor store right around the corner.' I rounded the corner but, by this time, there were only a few broken bottles and windows strewn about.

The entire stock was gone. That was only one store — there were several others. None were missed. I also came upon a furniture store on Barrington Street. The display windows were smashed and the furniture moved right out to the middle of the street. Cases of beer and liquor were stacked alongside chesterfields and chairs. I was invited to sit down and join in. I declined. I am not a prude and have done my share of drinking, but this type of behaviour was against my nature. Law and order were non-existent.

People were quick to blame the navy for these riots. Let me state right here, everybody was involved, civilians as well as the military. I saw a woman with a fur coat on her back and one draped over each arm and a civilian with wrist-watches from wrist to elbow on both arms. By the time the authorities realised they had lost all control, it was too late.

Police just stood idly by and watched. If I had been in their position I would have done exactly the same thing. What could they do?

I went back aboard the *Restigouche* shortly after. I had seen enough. That night I took over my watch as quartermaster. Part of the duties of a quartermaster was to stand guard on the gangway. I was instructed by the officer of the watch to frisk the crew coming back on board for loot. I went through the motions all right, but bearing in mind these fellows were my shipmates — I had to live with them in very close proximity — common sense prevailed. I will leave it at that. Word was that the RCMP would search the ships the next day. All night long you could hear the sound of splashing. Loot was being tossed overboard. I can still remember the sight of a sailor staggering aboard a nearby ship with a fully dressed mannequin in his arms. I thought at first it was a real woman. 'She' is still at the bottom of the Halifax harbour.

The riots went on for three days before order was restored. We were ordered out to sea and stayed clear of Halifax for many days, just sailing aimlessly around.

Never will I forget the sight of Barrington Street. There wasn't a pane of glass left for blocks.

Not all parties ended in a riot. Dame Anne Bryans was the commissioner for the British Red Cross Middle East Commission and was attending a party in Cairo on the evening of VE Day:

Late in the evening we heard the King's speech. It was a very great pleasure to all of us to be able to hear this with so many of our friends from home. I think that everyone in the Middle East was very homesick over the victory days. Everyone wanted to be at home and the accounts on the wireless of the celebrations in London did make us all want to be there. During the two days' holiday there was a magnificent race meeting staged by GHQ. This had camel, donkey and horse races and all units participated. A number of hospital patients came to the meeting and free tea was provided for everyone. The chief excitement was a donkey race, the jockeys being GHQ officers of the rank of brigadier and above, and everybody there highly enjoyed seeing all the generals competing.

In London, it seemed fitting that on 9 May the badly blitzed areas of the city should be hosts to the King and Queen. Large crowds turned out to give Their Majesties a warm welcome. It seemed a natural ending to a victory party and signalled that the time was drawing near when many loved ones would once again be united.

3

The Party's Over

*I*F MOST PEOPLE *woke up with a hangover on 9 May, their indulgence had certainly been justified. The years of doing without had finally ended and the future looked bright. The civilian population had experienced danger and knew the smell of death. Now it was time for them to reap the rewards.*

Crowds in the streets continued to move aimlessly about, not sure what was correct behaviour in peacetime. Twelve thousand people still saw the tube stations and deep shelters as their homes. Some, who had carried out duties in the civil defence, continued to visit their old warden posts or first-aid posts until they were closed down. Many of these civil defence clubs survived for years. For others, everything suddenly seemed flat, as if there were little to look forward to now that the war in Europe was finally over.

But for most, the main feeling was one of relief. Christine Pankhurst's uppermost thought was to get things back to normal once more:

The amazing thing was that I never met among the people, many friends and workmates, a feeling of despair. Yet many of us and them had lost everything – home, clothes, all belongings and often relatives dead or injured, three in our family. But among the people I knew all were glad to be alive and ready to start again. Of course many grieved for their dead and injured and were heartbroken, but as with most families that had suffered we were able to comfort each other.

Thousands of families prepared to welcome back those who had been absent. Along with the armed forces, yet to be demobbed, were almost 80,000 children who remained in the countryside. They were part of the 3.5 million evacuees who had been sent away from the inner cities and possible target areas for safety.

Some children who had been evacuated felt that life back with their parents would be one long party. Their return was all too often bitterly disappointing for them and for their parents, who now faced the daily routine of school hours and bedtimes. Some of the children were confused about who was who. Was the wonderful woman who had cared for them for so many years really 'Auntie' or 'Mum'? Children who had tasted the countryside missed the wonders of nature that had become familiar and found the city strange and frightening. Thousands revealed the shock of their uprooting through sleepwalking, nightmares and bedwetting. The disruption also meant that many of them were sadly behind in their education.

Pam Rendell (now Wood) had been evacuated in 1942 with other children from the Queen Elizabeth Hospital, Carshalton, Surrey, to Peckforten Castle, Cheshire:

My father had been taken prisoner in 1941 in Italy and so I had no contact with him until the end of the war.

At six and a half years old I was the youngest child at Peckforten and was also extremely shy. Imagine my horror when one day in May 1945 the matron called me to the front of the hall at morning prayers. She announced to everyone that a telegram had been sent for me to say that my father was coming home from the prisoner-of-war camp and would be coming soon to take me home. Everyone cheered but I just cried. I did not like being noticed.

A few days later both my parents came to collect me. My memories are of spending hours into the night on a crowded station platform at Chester waiting for a train with room on it to take us to London, then being squeezed into a crowded coach with my parents. London was a confusion of noise and dirt after living in the countryside for so long. I have no recollection of anything except another noisy, crowded station where we seemed to spend hours waiting for yet another train to take us to Yeovil in Somerset, which was our home. It was one very tired child that eventually arrived after over twenty-four hours of travelling to a house that I did not recognise and two sisters that I only vaguely remembered.

Monty Mazin was thirteen when he was evacuated from Stepney in the East End of London. He found himself in the small village of Totnes in Devon, where as a Jew he was something of an oddity:

I was with my brother, sister and mother. The only Jew in the area was a travelling salesman. No Jew had actually lived in the town. The family were split. I went in with complete strangers who were very nervous about taking a Jewish lad into the house. I was more fortunate than many Jewish children who were evacuated, as far as the Kosher food was concerned. A few years before I had contracted polio, which had resulted in long hospital stays where I had become accustomed to eating non-Jewish food. Mind you, when war had been declared the Chief Rabbi had broadcast to the nation's Jews that for the duration of the war Jews would be excused following their religious food habits.

I finally left when I was sixteen and found myself a job with the East London *Observer*. I was like a cub reporter. And then an astonishing thing happened. I got a call from the London *Evening News*, asking if I would cover the area of Stepney and Poplar during the V1 raids. And that, frankly, changed my life. I saw the horrors of war and the heroism and I guess the evacuation helped me not only to become a people person but I found it so much easier to speak to people who, for one thing, were not of the Jewish faith. I would have had a more difficult time if I had been kept within the confines of the Jewish area. Coming home for me was not only wonderful but I was made suddenly aware that I had spread my wings and would never be afraid to fly again to wherever I wanted to go.

Joan Murrell (now McCarthy), with her two sisters and brother, was evacuated to Loughborough, Leicestershire, at the beginning of the war:

I was the youngest sister, four years old. We remember the end of the war very much. It changed our lives completely and brought many tears. When war was declared my father joined the Royal Air Force and we remember it like it was yesterday. We used to be so proud of him in his uniform and we used to shine his buttons for him until they looked like gold.

My eldest sister was taken to a baker's shop in Loughborough to live with the family who owned it; my other sister and I were put in the house next door; and my brother went to a home nearby. We have many, many memories of this time. We were treated like their own and loved them in return. But, like all children at the time, we always looked forward to Dad coming home, but it was not to be.

While the war was on my parents were divorced. When war was over we never went home. My brother and I were put in a home in Essex and my sisters were taken to Canada. Our little world seemed to fall apart, believe me. Nothing could replace the emptiness of losing my sisters. I did not know where they were, nor them me. After many, many years of writing letters, I found my eldest sister. It had been thirty-nine years since I had seen her. I can't describe how we both felt. Three years ago we met for the first time since the end of the war. It is a strange feeling meeting someone who looks like you and even talks and walks the same. It's great, believe me. I have seen my other sister, too.

We never had the joy of seeing our father again. My mother had died and we knew nothing of our father's whereabouts. My sister and I set out to see if we could trace him and once again I wrote many, many letters. Can you imagine how we felt when we knew we had found the right name and place? But, once again, it was not to be. Our father had passed away two years before.

For many children, the end of the war meant a sad goodbye to those remarkable people who had acted as foster parents during their stay in the country. One Canadian couple had taken a six-year-old into their home in 1940:

My late husband and I were foster parents from early 1940 until June 1945. We took a girl of six and a half and she was almost twelve when she went back to England. Her last words, as she went down the escalator, were, 'I'll be back in ten years.' We kept in touch through the years and in 1955 she returned with a husband and two sons. Her first words were, 'I told you I'd be back in ten years.' They stayed with us until her husband got a job in Port Hope.

I am very proud of her. I have always felt having her was one of the best things my husband and I ever did, and feel amply rewarded for the time, sometimes difficult, many times a great joy.

Another Canadian family welcomed an evacuee from England into their home in 1939:

She was evacuated from London to Ontario. She was only six months younger than I and we were in the same grade at school. Mother dressed us alike, we did our homework together and went through all the difficult, formative years of twelve to almost eighteen. When the children were recalled in 1945, Alison [not her real name] was a month short of her eighteenth birthday and could not get permission from her parents to stay in Canada.

We were all heartbroken. Her greatest desire was to work and save enough money to come back. Her own parents were equally determined that she would not. Our letters were destroyed and she never received our gifts. Eventually she stopped writing. We hired a detective agency in England to trace her and found that she had run away from home less than a year after her return, then eloped and nobody knew her married name.

Every year we sent cards on her birthday and at Christmas. Finally we clicked around 1958. Alison's mother was ill and she had come home to help during Christmas week. She answered the door when the postman came and received our letters. She was overjoyed.

When she finally answered them, we were told that her family had made her believe that we had forgotten all about her after she went home and that was the reason for the absence of letters and gifts. She had been a mature working girl in Canada and they wanted her to stay home all day and look after her grandmother so her mother could go to work. She couldn't go out in the evening because her parents wanted to go to the pub. Thus, she had rebelled and left home, as she had returned to a culture that she no longer understood.

Michael Mansell was seven and a half when he was evacuated to New York City:

Finally VE Day came and the celebrations were hardly over before I was being readied for return to England. Sporting a new suit, a fancy watch and other things, I said my goodbyes once again and then joined fourteen other boys at the Barbizon Plaza Hotel, ready to be shipped home. It wasn't to be an ocean-going liner, but a brand-new invasion barge, LST 3514.

For the first three days we stayed tied up to the pier. There wasn't much to do to occupy ourselves, except to count the condoms floating in the stagnant water.

At long last we headed out to sea with a final wave to the Statue of Liberty. The two-week voyage had its exciting moments, but we made it safely to Plymouth. For me it was on to Paddington for the moment I'd been thinking a lot about. Would my parents know me in my long pants, wearing a fedora hat? Would they be like strangers? Well, I need not have worried on that score. I had been away a long time and it seemed strange at first, but I adjusted quickly. After all, I'd had quite a lot of practice.

Instead of waiting for the government to return the children to their homes, Ivy Edgington decided to go to Somerset to fetch hers and thank in person 'the super lady' who had given them so much care and affection:

This lady had accommodated me on several occasions when I had visited the children. It was very difficult for them to adjust to London, after years of country life, and to leave much-loved friends. My elder daughter had been with Mrs Norris for five years, from the age of five – the most formative years of a child's life. She was very sad, even with the end-of-war celebrations going on in the village. Mrs Norris, having no children of her own, had grown very fond of her and wanted to keep her.

I sometimes wish I had allowed this, as she had been so happy there and had left her heart. Even now, fifty years later, she still visits the village at every opportunity and hopes to retire there one day.

Of the twenty-four million males in the United Kingdom, 4,693,000 had been in uniform, nineteen per cent of the male population. A week after VE Day, Ernest Bevin, the Minister of Labour and National

Service, announced that military releases would begin on 18 June. By the end of the year it was hoped to have 750,000 service personnel back in civilian clothes.

Although the war with Japan had still to be won, the feeling was that this was now little more than a formality. In Britain it was time to look to the future and decide who was going to run the country once the coalition government had been put to pasture. An election held soon after the VE Day celebrations would, in the opinion of most people, certainly see Churchill and the Conservatives returned to power. For obvious reasons, the Labour and Liberal Parties were not as anxious as the Conservatives for this to happen, and urged that the elections be delayed as long as possible. After the emergence of a 'caretaker government' and weeks of heated debate in the House of Commons, an election was called for 5 July. An astonished world heard the result. Churchill had been thrown aside in favour of the Labour Party, led by Clement Attlee.

It is not difficult to understand what had happened. In the aftermath of war, many of the British electorate felt they deserved a new life, and chose a government that would favour the poor and middle classes. Certainly lack of housing played a large part in determining the way people voted, as thousands whose homes had been destroyed made their way to the polls alongside members of the armed forces.

The election over, all eyes turned to the Far East. Families of those still being held prisoner had heard horrendous stories of cruelty and were sure that, if the war with Japan did not end soon, they would never see their loved ones again. Those serving in the area were just as eager to see an end to the conflict. Some had fought their way through Europe before being posted to the East, and had no desire to face another enemy, wherever it may be.

Then on 6 and 9 August, the use of atomic bombs on Hiroshima and Nagasaki – the most powerful weapons the world had ever seen – persuaded the Japanese to surrender.

For the second time in three months, the British had occasion to celebrate. Showers of paper poured from office buildings in London on to the heads of those below. But once more the news was not made official immediately and the premature parties fizzled out as people waited for word from the Prime Minister. It finally came at midnight on 14 August, when the BBC asked listeners to stand by for a special announcement. Most people were in bed and did not hear the news until a repeat of the broadcast at seven o'clock the next morning.

33

The party spirit spread slowly, perhaps because many people were unaware that the day had been declared a holiday until they arrived at work. Many workers were trapped in a reverse rush hour as they hurried back home. An official request that the reported Japanese surrender be treated with reserve was ignored and, as on VE Day, Piccadilly Circus soon became the hub of the assembling crowds. Dancing started but was soon abandoned as the dancers ran out of space.

15 August was also the day set aside for the state opening of the new Labour-dominated Parliament. The King and Queen drove to Westminster in an open carriage, apparently unconcerned about the light rain that was falling. The normally small crowds gathering for such an event had swelled, with people no doubt hoping for a repeat of the celebrations that had marked VE Day.

Marcia Vardon remembers the period well:

When VJ Day finally arrived in the August of that year, it was my twenty-first birthday and I was in London with two friends. So we were caught up with the celebrations and general rejoicing, like the dancing and singing in Trafalgar Square. I remember how we talked in the train coming back home to the West Country as to what the future would bring for us and everybody else. Plymouth had been heavily bombed, the city centre destroyed, thousands of homes and countless lives lost, so there would have to be a time of great rebuilding. Sometimes, in the months that lay ahead, it was hard to believe that the war really was over. The promised brave new world seemed a long time coming.

One naval officer remembers being in Portsmouth on VJ Day. His ship, a frigate, was tied up alongside a sister ship. The celebration for both ships started about mid-morning:

An RNR officer was well 'bombed' by noon. About that time, we observed him crossing the gangplank to the jetty with his arms rigidly extended, carrying in both hands duty-free bottles of liquor – in one hand was certainly scotch, in the other he had anything from scotch to whatever was left in the wardroom stock.

He walked through the dockyard – half a mile or more – to the dockyard gates, where the police and officers of HM Customs were always looking for attempts to smuggle dutiable goods, especially liquor, ashore. They paid him no attention and one would assume that he was going to find a congenial party somewhere in Portsmouth to share his wealth. Some two hours later he returned to his ship still carrying the two bottles, still unopened, in his hands at the ends of his extended arms. He retired to his cabin and I know not when he surfaced.

Norman Ellison was in the Royal Observer Corps and lived on Merseyside from 1939 to 1945. The following extract from his diary describes a totally different scene when the war with Japan finally came to an end:

16 August/45: VJ Day: Victory over Japan Day and a public holiday. Went down to West Kirkby in the morning and found council women putting up flags in a half-hearted manner. No signs of joy, of enthusiasm, no cheering crowds, all shops shut and the streets almost deserted. I could not help but contrast this feeling of apathy with the day peace was declared at the end of the First World War, when the streets of Manchester were packed to suffocation by delirious crowds . . . Maybe most of us are mentally and physically exhausted; maybe we have become so accustomed to living under warlike restraints, we have not yet realised that fighting has stopped. I can speak only for myself on this day. I feel no elation, no uplifting of spirit, only a sort of dumb, inarticulate thankfulness that the hell of war, the killing, the misery is over; that Anne and I are alive and well.

At night we went to Caldy Hill to see the bonfires blazing on the distant Welsh hills. What pleased us more was to see the opposite side of the Dee twinkling with thousands of streetlamps and lighted windows. So we went home, opened wide the curtains and switched on every light in the house. More than anything else did this action . . . bring home to us the fact that the war had ended.

For those still in the Far East the greatest relief was felt by the POWs. The following note was found after the war. It was dated 17 August 1945, with an address, Tamuan Camp, Thailand. It was written in pencil on paper made of banana leaves:

We are free at last, last night we had our first concert and the camp RSM announced it from the stage it was a scene I shall never forget every national anthem was sung + cheering terrific they even put the Union Jack on the lookout post at 10 p.m. they said that only the firing had stopped + no papers signed + we were still under their control they think two weeks the latest for our chaps to get here so all are hoping home for Xmas can't write much more too excited had 3½ yrs of hell.

Oss Luce was sent from Canada to England with the air force in January 1941. He was single and twenty years old. He was later posted to Singapore, where he was captured by the Japanese in March 1942.

At the end of the war we were back in Singapore. The Japs toured us around wherever they needed slave labour and, at that time, we had returned to Singapore. We were sitting there waiting for them to clear the mines so that they could get us out, out of the straits. It was just a little bit of a joke. We said what we should do now, we have to settle down, we have to get married. The most popular choice would be a blonde, deaf-and-dumb nymphomaniac. That was the consensus of opinion.

There were seven of us Canadians – we didn't all make it – but those of us who did make it back came home together on the *Queen Elizabeth*.

We landed in Halifax and we had to go to the pool in Lachine, outside of Montreal – and whoever had the embarkation orders for that had a sense of humour. Here were two guys (the other fellow was considerably older than myself) and we hadn't been with women for four years and they put us on a trainload of WDs, the WAAFs. Two of us on a trainload of 550 WAAFs! We were so nervous we didn't know what the heck to do. Talk about a virgin on the verge! It was like Rip Van Winkle coming out. You see, we hadn't been allowed any means of communication, no letters, no nothing. We came into a different world when we returned to Canada. It was unbelievable. It was like the yokel going to New York City or something like that – staring at everything, everything was new. I was twenty-six. I had been in prison for three and a half years.

You're at a loss for answers. Looking back on the experience now it was very unsettling. The group of us that had gone over in 1941 had been put on to radar, and I just came off the Official Secrets Act in June 1990. Everything we knew had to be kept quiet and a lot of what we knew had to be memorised. So, consequently, when we got captured, here we were with the secrets of radar in our noggins and we were afraid that somebody was going to spill the beans that we knew something.

I remember thinking that I would sneak in on my mum and dad and not let them know I was coming home. When we got to Lachine I had made a date with a couple of the girls we'd come up from Halifax with to go out that night, but two of the service police came and got me, along with the minister, and put me on a train out of Lachine and sent me home. I must confess although I was anxious to get home I would have liked to have kept the date.

The minister phoned my mother and he said I was on the train was only one stop between Lachine and Toronto, so in Toronto I should get off the train. To top it all off, on the train I met up with this young lady – she was a good-looking gal – and I was debating in my head, do I make a pass or do I try to get home or what do I do? We were walking out of the station and I was told I was being paged in the R T O office, so that ended that one. My parents had driven to Toronto from St Catharines to meet me.

All the neighbours from the block where I lived were in our house when I got home at 7 a.m. It was quite a noisy place for a while.

As the American-Japanese peace signing date of 28 August approached, the Americans moved into the area of the official surrender. American prisoners of war near Tokyo were astonished to see a landing craft with Marines aboard coming ashore. A member of Admiral Halsey's staff, Harold Stassen, stepped out and up to the prison gate. The Japanese commandant stopped him. 'I have no authority to turn these men over to you,' he said. Stassen pushed him to one side. 'You have no authority, period,' he retorted.

The Stars and Stripes flew at the yardarm of the USS Missouri. The American dignitaries stood on deck waiting for the Japanese. At 8.56 a.m. they arrived aboard the destroyer Lansdown. The embarrassment of surrender was only equalled by Japanese Foreign Minister

Shigemitsu's difficulty in climbing the ship's ladder. Years before, an assassin's bomb had blown off his leg. His wooden replacement had never been a good fit. It was rumoured that the prosthesis had been given to him by the Emperor and he had to wear it, even though he was in great pain.

Shigemitsu limped forward and sat down in a chair facing the surrender documents. One was in English and the other in Japanese. After marking the Japanese characters of his name, General MacArthur signed on behalf of the Allied powers. When everyone had signed, MacArthur made his way to a microphone and broadcast to the American people. For them, World War II was officially over.

Two weeks later the British met the Japanese in Singapore for their signing. On 12 September, Louis Mountbatten, supreme Allied commander in South East Asia, accepted the formal surrender of all Japanese forces in the region and brought to an end the most destructive war in the history of mankind.

The priority was now to demobilise what many had termed 'The Forgotten Army'. Even before the Japanese surrender, the Cunard liner Scythia *had set sail from Bombay carrying a large number of Britain's Fourteenth Army, including Gord Godfrey, a Canadian:*

Excitement on the ship was everything you might imagine. *Bless 'em all* echoed across Bombay. Shades of Kipling's *Big Drunk Draf'*.

The fun died quickly when we boarded. *Scythia* was built for the North Atlantic. Pre-war North Atlantic ships of *Scythia*'s class didn't have air-conditioning. Our ship had virtually no forced air circulation either. We expected life to improve when we sailed and created a breeze, but we got a lesson in tropical meteorology.

We got fog, as thick a fog as I ever saw. Made with the hot water from the Arabian Sea. And we got a dead calm. Anyone who had escaped prickly heat before got it now. We slowly poked our way toward the Red Sea.

Someone discovered that a cardboard box stuck through a porthole made a reasonable air scoop. Soon every porthole had a carton. In the captain's words, the ship looked like a garbage scow. Better a garbage scow with air circulating than a trim, airless, North Atlantic liner.

About the time we groped our way out of the fog and began to move a little faster toward the Red Sea, the radio announced that the Americans had dropped the world's biggest bomb on Japan. Those Americans – always the biggest of everything, especially lies. We roared with laughter.

A day or two later the Americans improved their joke by announcing a second bomb and that they expected the Japanese to surrender immediately. And then they did surrender. And there we were, heading up the Red Sea, halfway between nowhere and nowhere else. The world's biggest party coming up and we were going to miss it.

And we did miss it. On VJ Day the *Scythia* poked through the Suez Canal. All the cardboard ventilators had been scrapped on the order of the captain, who refused to sail the ship within sight of his equals looking as it had.

There was no joy on that ship. There was no booze on that ship either. The ultimate blow came from the BBC. Their broadcaster, covering the celebrations in London, moved from pub to pub around Piccadilly catching the laughter and the sound of the beer pumps in each and transmitting a deadly accurate reproduction to the middle of the Suez Canal. And the ship's loudspeakers ensured we heard it all. Bone dry, in temperatures well over a hundred degrees, we listened to the suds and the parties. And each burst of bubbles was met with a massive universal groan.

By the time the *Scythia* got to England, 'coming home' was passé.

Ken Booth was a former flight lieutenant with the Royal Canadian Air Force who found it even more difficult to get home:

My coming home, I thought, was to start early in February of 1945, when I had completed one and a half tours of operations and at least one tour of non-ops. In fact, my return took six more months before it was complete.

My locale was Bengal, my role air navigator trained in the RCAF, but attached to the RAF. My posting came through, but it was another tour of non-ops, this time in Calcutta. The only saving grace of this was that it gave me the opportunity, for the first time since leaving England, to talk with a Canadian liaison officer. His immediate reaction was, 'According to our records you went home

long ago. Just hold on and I will get back to you.' True to his word
he did and by early April I was in Bombay waiting for a troop ship to
England.

Finally, we boarded (I believe it was the *Stratheden*) and the
approximately three-week trip was more or less uneventful. The
European war was nearly over, and we were allowed to smoke on
deck through the Red Sea and the Mediterranean. Coming up the
Irish Sea some of the accompanying frigates did drop some depth
charges, but I suspect it was just celebrating the end of the war in
Europe. We arrived near Glasgow on 7 May.

The next day, 8 May, was my birthday and also V E Day, so over
the years I have never forgotten when the war in Europe ended. I
had reached London by noon of that day and was in the crowds in
Piccadilly Circus, and in others lined up six deep at the bars. Later
that afternoon I was in Bournemouth.

The conventional wisdom was that you would be checked in,
immediately sent on leave and called back within a few days to get
shipped home. That was the way it had been and the way it started
for us. But we did not get the call back, so we slowly drifted back to
find out what was wrong. The P O Ws were being brought back and
they had priority once they were fit to travel. We could not argue
about the justice of his, but it was obviously going to delay our own
repatriation. May dragged on with its inevitable flight parades and
other square-bashing, but mostly ennui. Rumours began floating
around that anyone who signed up for service in the Pacific would
get priority on the ships, but those of us who had been there did not
want to sign up to serve once again in that hell-hole. June came and
went and our resolve wavered, with no hope of seeing a ship to take
us home. Finally, about mid-July, we said, 'What the hell. O K, I'll
sign,' and it was not long before we were headed for Liverpool and
the *Strathearn* for our trip home.

The Atlantic late that July was a pussycat – bright sunshine and
the water so calm that, at times, it was like a mill pond and you
could see the clouds reflected in it. That was a fine trip.

As we neared the end, we heard first a rumour and then an official
announcement that we would not be going to Halifax, but instead
would head up the St Lawrence to Quebec. We may have been the
first troop ship to do so. This meant further delay, but so what? I

particularly recall the late afternoon when we entered the wide mouth of the river and could see the north shore. The rail was lined with troops gazing more or less in silence when suddenly, on shore, there was a puff of steam and then the deep whistle of a Canadian train. There was a spontaneous roar from everyone – at last it sounded like they were near home.

It was probably 28 July when we arrived in Quebec City to the news that we would not disembark until the following morning – another delay. We were greeted by large crowds and welcoming speeches all in French, which were incomprehensible to practically all. We then travelled by train, eventually, to Montreal, where my fiancée, to whom I had become engaged three years before, was waiting. Frenzied preparations followed and a week later we were married and off on our honeymoon by train to Vancouver, where my parents were. While there the first incomprehensible news about the atomic bombs on Hiroshima and Nagasaki came through. Then, about mid-August, we took the boat to Victoria and, just as we disembarked, every bell and whistle in town, every taxi and car, began to make a raucous noise. For a few minutes we wondered what had happened, but very soon realised it could only mean the end of the war with Japan.

That was the moment I really felt I had finally come home. And that was the time I told my new wife that I had signed up for a further tour, against my best judgement.

Every form of transport was called upon to get those serving overseas back home. Naval vessels, including aircraft carriers, which had been filled with crews in white uniforms suddenly found their decks covered in khaki as troops by the thousands crowded on board. But there was never enough transport available for those waiting at the embarkation points. Margaret Barklem (now Cook) was a WAAF stationed in Tel Litwinsky, near Tel Aviv:

We were fed up with waiting but, when one thinks about it afterwards, what a colossal job it must have been to ship thousands of troops to the UK from overseas. Before leaving, the fellows were called to the office and interviewed by the adjutant, who asked if they would join up for extra time. One wag was heard to say, 'After this racket I wouldn't join two pieces of string.' Following a lengthy time in the service, I would imagine that one would cease to think for oneself, being continually reminded that, in the service, 'You are not paid to think, you're paid to do as you are told.' Who wants that for any longer than necessary?

Finally, it came to my turn and I left Number 3 in July 1946 for the transit camp at Almaza, Egypt. As the fellows used to say, we were now ready to 'fall in and face the boat, kit-bags on the right AND stop crying you in the rear rank or you won't go home.'

A week later we had to re-mark our kit ready for the next boat, being told it had only twenty-nine places for WAAFs aboard. As there were fifty of us waiting, I kept my fingers crossed and, this time, was lucky. The *Otranto* had picked up troops from Hong Kong, Singapore and Ceylon, apart from the Middle East. Evidently they had had a rough trip in the Far East, running into a monsoon in the Indian Ocean. However, the first five days aboard was like a cruise to me. A sweepstake was run on the number of miles travelled each day. We passed Algiers on the Monday and Gibraltar on the Tuesday and, as we went through the Straits at 9 a.m., we had an excellent view of the Rock, most people being on deck with their cameras.

On the last lap of the journey home my feelings were somewhat mixed. I did not know what to expect on arrival in the UK. We had continually heard disquieting tales about 'Blighty' and one wondered just what changes had taken place during that couple of years. How was the job situation? the food? what of the family? etc. How the devil was I going to settle down again? How on earth was I going to acclimatise to the weather, the rationing of food and clothing, the shortage of everything? Above all, how would things go with David and myself after a two-year parting? I wondered whether one or the other had changed and, if so, for better or worse. What had time in the service done to or for us? What did the future hold?

I then decided all those things could wait. It did not seem that I had been away for two years. The time had sort of closed in and I felt that it was only yesterday that I had been on my way overseas. I felt that I would never have any regrets over all about service in the ME, except perhaps that I never reached Cyprus. I was the eldest of four children – life had not been easy at home – so, without a doubt, I had just experienced the most carefree time of my life.

I had written home from Almaza, giving the name of the ship on which I would be travelling, not knowing what was going to happen on arrival. When we reached Southampton David was on the dock, not in uniform but in grey pants and his new sports jacket, made in Poona. The troop ship was packed with personnel for release into civilian life, hundreds hanging over the rails at their first glimpse of the UK for some time. I guess the checked sports jacket David was wearing gave the impression of his being a bookmaker, as some of the fellows were shouting to him, 'I'll have two bob on Black Beauty,' and comments of that kind. Little did they realise that he had just been demobilised, having been in uniform like them a few days previously.

As it would take some time to organise our orderly departure from the ship, an officer okayed my request to go down to the dock for a while by giving me a pass to present to those guarding the exit. I ran down the gangplank into David's arms to the cheers of hundreds of troops.

4

A Stranger at the Door

*T*HE TRUE REWARD *for those fortunate enough to have loved ones returning was, of course, a face-to-face meeting. For those whose sons had survived, the happiness and anticipation were pure and simple: their children were coming back from the war. But for a young wife who had waved her husband goodbye years ago, there was cause for some concern. Many wartime marriages had taken place within weeks of the couple's meeting. How much would the young stranger she had taken to her bed have changed in the intervening years? And, just as important, what changes would the returning hero see in his wife, and how would he feel about them? These questions would have to remain unanswered until the fateful knock on the door.*

Enid Innes-Ker's husband Tam had been a POW and as her hopes rose when the end of the war was approaching, she and her friends began to think about the prospect of their husbands returning:

We all found ourselves thinking that we ought to brush up on our cooking – in my case I needed to learn from scratch. I did learn something of use about cooking procedures and slightly got over my feeling of fear and lack of self-confidence at doing anything in the kitchen. I still have some of those recipes, most of which seem to need the use of reconstituted eggs!

When VJ Day finally arrived on 15 August they decided to miss the celebrations:

Maw and I did not feel like going up to town and joining in the junketing. We were still stunned by the speed with which the war had ended and it seemed more a time for quiet thought and thankfulness . . . I was tremendously relieved, I was terribly excited, and I was also somewhat apprehensive. The moment of truth lay not very far ahead; had my husband, Tam, survived, how was his health, and how had these years as a Japanese POW changed him?

The morning after Tam had arrived home safely there was a shock:

I emerged from my bath to find that Tam had disappeared. When he did appear he was bearing a bouquet of flowers for me. Not finding a flower shop nearby he had hopped on a bus, and, of course, automatically proffered a penny. The combination of Tam's uniform, his bright yellow face, the fact that he did not know the minimum fare was now 1½d and that he was seeking flowers for his wife bowled over the conductress. She would not accept a fare from him, told him where to get off and find a flower shop, helped him down with care and sent him on his way wishing him luck.

Once they had survived the first year of their husbands' absence, many women had managed to adapt to their new, single status. Now they had to adapt again.
   Kit Beasley lived on the Isle of Dogs in London. She had married in 1941 and waited from 1942 to 1946 for her husband to return from the war:

I can remember my husband coming home from Egypt. I was in bed and it was early in the morning, about 7.30, and he was knocking at the door and I looked out and I thought, oh, my God, he's home . . . It was a mixed feeling because I'd made so many friends and I knew very well that from then on I was going to be at home.
   At first we used to argue – but gradually we worked it out. We had to, we just had to work it out. You had to learn all about one another again because obviously we'd both changed in that time . . . I was more grown up, I'd gone around.
   When he came out it was very, very difficult to get to know him again. I think it was a time when we could have easily split up. The

first year that he was away I sort of pined, but after that I thought, he's gone and so I just led the normal life of a young girl. He came home and no way did I feel I could settle down with him. You had to go all through a sort of courtship again. Four years is a very long time to be apart, but gradually we got together, though things were very, very difficult because we had nothing. Our money from the army was very little and we had just the necessary things like a bed and a chair – no carpets or things like that. The island was just like a bomb site after the war. My home was bombed during the war. We finally found an old flat. It had an outside toilet, no bathroom. Times were very hard. It was heartbreaking to see the bombing on the Isle of Dogs, especially Cubitt Town. That was very badly bombed. There were just prefab houses for the homeless to live in.

May Smith remembers that the initial awkwardness of her reunion with her husband didn't last long:

You don't know what to say at first. You've got such a lot of things to say, you just cry. It's so wonderful that everything's over. You feel that if you've got over the war you can get over anything.

My husband had missed the baby; he'd missed those little first bits and pieces that children do. It was very traumatic for him.

We had to stay with my mother-in-law. You know, being a Cockney you can always find something to make a joke about. My mother-in-law insisted on giving up their very old bed. We were just so exhausted after my husband returned home, we just went to sleep. We'd talked our heads off and it was about two o'clock in the morning when we finally got to bed. And suddenly this bed just slid off the frame and left us standing upright! We looked at one another and just couldn't stop laughing. My husband said to me, 'If you're waiting for the Number 8 bus, it doesn't come through here,' to sort of break the tension. We giggled all night long. We just couldn't stop laughing. His brothers were in the other room and the next morning at breakfast they were all saying. 'What the devil did you get up to last night, you two?'

Karina Powell was married in 1945. Her husband was in the army from 1944 to 1947, serving in India and Singapore. They exchanged letters every day:

I do not know what we talked about. Every day during the evening I would write a six to ten page letter.

It was 5 November 1947, Bonfire Night, when my husband was demobbed. No telephones in those days in private homes, unless you were very rich. I received a letter a fortnight before, giving me the date he was leaving Colchester, which was 5 November. For a fortnight I sat knitting a pullover as a surprise gift, every night from 6 p.m. until 11 p.m. the pins would clang, clang, my fingers really ached. I watched all the fireworks at the local church bonfire from my bedroom window.

It was about 11 p.m. I was so tired waiting for the bell to ring, I fell asleep and about 6 a.m. I felt his arms around me and heard the words, 'Darling, I'm home with you at last.'

We cried and our emotions were terrific. We could not believe it was true. We were so happy. Inside his kit-bag were presents, handbag in crocodile skin, nylons, sweets . . . It seemed never-ending. It was just like Father Christmas coming. Yes, he had a beard, too, and looked like one.

On the following day, John informed me that he had two bags at the station. Well, I could not believe it. One kit-bag full of all my letters and the other one contained tins of peaches (large tins, about twenty). They had been brought all the way from Singapore. It was peaches every meal for some weeks.

We had a holiday in the Lake District – our belated honeymoon. We bought a house and we were so very happy. I really think John being away made us grow much closer to each other. He always said he would never leave me again, and he never did. Unfortunately he died of cancer six years ago, and his last words were, 'Well, love, we have been so happy. I made it through the war and never have we been apart since my duty was done.'

These are the happy memories I live with. If only I had only three years to wait again, life would be complete.

The wartime routine became more than just acceptable for some – it became enjoyable. One woman has only sad memories of life after her husband's return:

Sadly our relationship changed as a result of his homecoming. I was happy and contented while he was away. I was working as a nursing sister in a hall hospital.

He was demobbed in October 1945, by which time we had a baby daughter whom he hadn't seen. I really thought that I'd be left out in the cold while he fussed over the baby. Alas, no. He was insanely jealous of her and told me I should be cuddling him, not the baby.

We did manage to buy a house, but could only furnish half of it. By then we had three children. I couldn't stand scrounging and scraping any longer. I decided to go back to work on part-time night duty. I had hoped he would help me by getting up earlier in the morning, get the baby washed and fed. No, he didn't do a damn thing to help me.

However, after thirty-five years of marriage, four children and a nice home, he deserted me for a mistress twenty years his junior. After sharing the hard times and bringing up four children, I had looked forward to our retirement together. I only wish we had never come back from World War II.

When her husband went away, Cordelia Holman would have described him as a kind and loving man. Her views changed after he returned:

Before the war my husband was absolutely great and was a loving father to our young son. He had been a regimental sergeant-major in the Ordnance Corps. When he returned from four years in India, he came back arrogant and self-opinionated. He did not want our son and suggested I hire babysitters so that we could go out each night. From then until he died of lung cancer in 1980, he had affairs with other women.

His father advised me to leave him. He said he was his son, but he would never be any good to me. But I still loved him and he still came home at night, although he took his latest lady to Spain on holiday three times. So I am afraid I felt the war had ruined my marriage.

I nursed him through his last illness and when he died I told our vicar I would only feel a sense of release. He said it was very understandable in the circumstances. How, nearly eleven years on, at times I miss the love we once had.

Elsie Moyer's husband was called up in 1940. They had been married in December 1939 and had had a few months together before he left for North Africa:

He was in the desert until he was captured at Tobruk with a few thousand others and spent three and a half years in various POW camps in Italy and then Germany.

One Monday morning I went to work as usual and, during the afternoon, I received a phone call from the girl I shared a house with in Balham, South London. She said that Ralph, my husband, had just arrived in a taxi and would I come home at once. She put him on the phone and he just shouted so loudly. Apparently he had been in a camp with 2000 other POWs, hence the shouting.

I cannot describe my feelings on that journey home. I had always planned in my mind to be all dressed up on the day he came home and there I was in my working 'lot'.

When we met he looked so poorly. He was yellow and it turned out that he had marched 300 miles across Germany in the winter, sleeping rough in the open all the time and with no proper meals. He had not had his boots off for six weeks.

The Yanks released them and flew them home to an airfield in Oxford, where they were deloused and given new uniforms and a roast beef dinner and then the next day put on the train for Paddington.

He was given six weeks' leave and double rations. I discovered that if I took him shopping with me all sorts of things appeared that we rarely saw: liver, eggs, sausages, etc.

The first night home he talked, or shouted, all night. No romance or anything of that kind, in spite of my super nightie.

We went away to a guest-house in Brixham for a holiday. It was rather funny. He used to dive into the nearest baker's shop and come out with a large cake, which he used to devour during the night, leaving me to get rid of the crumbs.

He was much more aggressive than he used to be. One day on a train, two ladies got on, took one look at him (he was in civvies) and started talking in loud voices that it was all right for some, how did they get away with not being called up, etc. He blew his top, showed them his repatriation papers and they apologised.

Thinking about it all now, I don't think he ever really got back to his old self. The war did something to him, apart from giving him an ulcer. His political views had changed somewhat. Also, he flatly refused to accept his medals and, when they arrived, he sent them straight back with a curt note.

Troops who had served in areas prone to tropical disease suffered yet another strain on their marriage. For Rosina Smith, who was married in 1940, her husband's illness, in a strange way, helped them to recapture the love they once had:

I went to his home in London and he was called up in May 1941. Our son Martin was born a month after he sailed for the Far East. He landed in Singapore and was taken prisoner on 15 February 1942.

I looked for the post each morning. Sundays were always a blank day – no post – but I went to early service and that's what kept me going during the three and a half years he was a prisoner. I wrote to other wives of POWs and we kept our hopes going. Also, many wives and mothers called in the shop to talk to me, saying they got strength from me as I was always so sure he'd come back.

15 August 1945 was a great day. I was awakened by a neighbour throwing stones at the bedroom window. Bonfires were blazing all around. Martin wakened with all the excitement and asked what was the matter. I said, 'The war's over, darling.' He said, 'Then my daddy will come home now.' The last all clear sounded, tears of joy falling fast.

The next days that followed I just couldn't settle. I was on pins all the time and quite bad-tempered. I'd arranged a holiday with a friend and her two little girls. I only stayed away four days, I couldn't settle. In case there was any post I spent the rest of the week at home. I took Martin out for walks but, if I saw anyone coming along the road that I knew, I'd look the other way or, if possible, turn down another road so I wouldn't have to speak to them. Being a small village, everyone more or less knew of Steve and, of course, wanted to know if I'd heard any news. It was always no. By the weekend I'd come down with the flu, so I did not go to work on Monday, Tuesday or Wednesday (9–11 September).

Martin brought me the post on Wednesday and he held an OHMS letter and a small pencil-written note. I grabbed the note. It was dated 31 August 1945, just saying, 'Happy. Well. Longing reunion. Love, Smith.' I forgot my flu. I shot out of bed and ran downstairs and threw my arms around my gran and shouted, 'He's alive, he's alive!' She said, 'Don't cry, love,' and we both had tears rolling down our cheeks.

All the village rejoiced. I hoisted the Union flag, then sent telegrams to his mum and family in London. He was in hospital for a few days in Rangoon, being checked and kitted out. He took three weeks to get home. He landed in Liverpool one foggy day, 12 October 1945. My dream boat was the SS *Boisevane*, a Dutch ship.

Then all the doubts came crowding in. Will he still love and want me? Have I changed? What will he think of Martin? How will he talk to a little boy, almost four years old, he's never seen?

On Sunday 14 October at four o'clock, the double-decker bus stopped outside our gate. Martin had been waiting all day by the gate. The khaki-clad figure was being helped off the bus with all his kit. 'Welcome home, darling' just came out and all the bus passengers witnessed our meeting. No doubts at all at that moment. Martin couldn't take his eyes off him. He couldn't speak till Daddy pulled a football out of his kit-bag, then he didn't stop talking. While having tea, Martin just sat looking at his daddy. Steve said, 'What's wrong, son?' Martin said, 'You fascinate me.' What a big word for a little lad just a fortnight short of his fourth birthday.

On 16 October Steve had his first attack of malaria. I hadn't a clue what to do, but our local doctor was wonderful. The bouts of malaria came every three weeks and I had to learn to cope with them and the bad temper that came just before each bout. I was certainly thrown in the deep end, but it helped to clear any doubts either of us had about each other. It cemented our marriage, especially when nine months and ten days later Clifford was born. Clatterbridge Hospital's first rice baby, Steve used to call him. Clifford certainly was sent for a purpose. He brought Steve back to sanity and helped him to understand his four-year-old son better.

Of course, many husbands did not come back. Elizabeth Reynolds was married in 1941, at the age of twenty-one. Three months later her husband left for overseas duty. The following year, the day after their anniversary, their baby son was born:

People don't realise how precious it is for a young father to hold a baby and I feel to this day that my son missed out on this. To me it would be worth all the money in the world just to have had my husband hold the baby.

I got the telegram on 20 July 1944. I had been over at my mother's and I had just got back and the knock came at the door. It was a Red Cross woman, a stranger, who just handed me a telegram reporting that my husband was killed.

I was living with my husband's mother when the war ended. Everyone was rejoicing in the streets and I can remember the church bells ringing and everybody was happy. But my little son and I were standing looking out the window and I was crying, yet I was happy the war was over. I was so sad that his father wasn't coming back. But then, you had to pick up the pieces and go on with life and make a good life for my child. It was hard.

Betty Davies's husband had been a prisoner in Singapore. In 1945 his ship arrived in Southampton and two days later he stepped off a train in Liverpool:

There was quite a crowd, not just friends and relatives, waiting at Lime Street Station as the POW train arrived. When Ben (my husband) saw me, he dropped the two kit-bags he was carrying, took me in his arms and kissed me, oblivious of the onlookers. One old lady standing nearby picked up one of the kit-bags and said, 'Aw, God 'elp 'im – you can tell she's 'is.'

That was a wonderful homecoming, but what was to follow was years of intermittent illness. His eyes were damaged as a result of malnutrition and ill treatment. Five years ago Ben was declared legally blind.

Anne Cutler spent five and a half years waiting for her husband to return. He had gone to England from Canada just before Christmas 1939, leaving her with three little boys to care for:

In 1945 special trains began bringing the troops back to Britain. Waiting eagerly on the platforms to greet them were the loved ones they had left behind.

Warm embraces set the ball rolling
as reunited couples embark on the
sometimes delicate process of
getting to know each other again.

Brightly coloured bunting welcomes this sergeant back to the home in South London that he has not seen for nearly five years.

Back from Burma, a soldier is accompanied home from the station by his joyful family.

The luxury of being home again.
Many family celebrations continued
for weeks.

Above: Ecstatic: the first US servicemen to be demobilised, April 1945.

Below: Sunny smiles as members of the ATS arrive at Regent's Park Barracks for demobilisation.

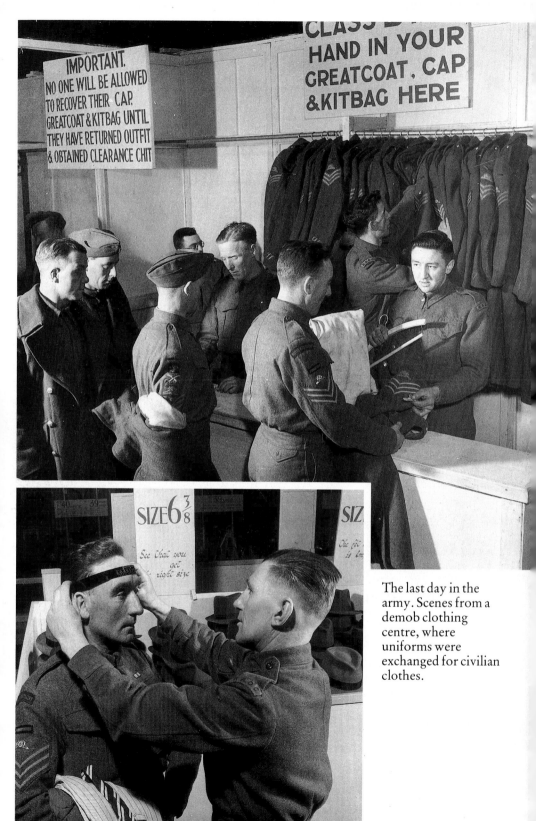

IMPORTANT.
NO ONE WILL BE ALLOWED
TO RECOVER THEIR CAP.
GREATCOAT & KITBAG UNTIL
THEY HAVE RETURNED OUTFIT
& OBTAINED CLEARANCE CHIT

CLASS B
HAND IN YOUR
GREATCOAT, CAP
& KITBAG HERE

SIZE 6⅜

See that you
get right size

The last day in the
army. Scenes from a
demob clothing
centre, where
uniforms were
exchanged for civilian
clothes.

The abrupt return to civilian life was not always easy for men who had grown accustomed to life in the forces.

A demobbed officer is shown the ropes on the first day of his new job in the sales department of a London firm.

Ex-servicemen and former prisoners-of-war attend classes as part of their training to become taxi-drivers, above, and bus conductors, below.

I didn't know at the time I was carrying our fourth child. Somehow we got through the years. Certainly I never suffered from lack of food. I inherited a little money from my grandmother in 1943, which enabled me to put a down payment on a house in Galt, Ontario, and I worked in a shoe factory part-time, so managed quite well.

The war ended in May and on 15 June I had a telegram from my husband that he had landed in Halifax and would be home shortly. I contacted the Red Cross and they said they would see that I was at the train station when he arrived. On the 17th, Father's Day, there was a rap at my front door about noon hour and a gentleman asked if I was Mrs Cutler and said there was someone out in his car who wanted to see me. As I ran down the street I could see two army hats and knew it had to be him. The whole street got to see the homecoming, as it was a nice day and people were sitting out. The man he was with had picked up my husband and a buddy hitchhiking. They had got off the train a few stops early and hitchhiked the rest of the way. The good Samaritan enjoyed the reunion.

In the autumn of 1941, a sixteen-year-old Canadian schoolgirl named Susanne Porter met a nineteen-year-old soldier. In the next four months the soldier managed to get leave three times. The friendship flourished:

Then came embarkation leave and a long period of silence before the first letters from 'somewhere in Britain' arrived. For four years letters crossed the Atlantic to and from Britain and then, after D-Day, from northern Europe. I graduated from high school and enlisted in the Canadian Women's Army Corps and the letters continued – hundreds, I guess. Finally, on New Year's Eve 1946, a telegram was delivered to the CWAC barracks in Ottawa: 'Arrived in Halifax. See you soon. Love.' The long wait was almost over. Then came a telephone call from his mother. He was very ill and could not travel. Would the girl he was anxious to meet again travel to meet him? Of course she would!

As usual, I was broke, but army friends are good friends, as they proved to be when they all chipped in to get me on my way. My commanding officer issued a furlough pass and I was on my way to meet my soldier. What a trip! The train was stuck in snowdrifts for ten hours, meaning that the ferry had left when we got to Saint John. There was an anxious CWAC and an even more anxious soldier, fearing he had been stood up. After a night in a strange CWAC barracks and then an early morning crossing on a stormy Bay of Fundy, I finally took the train from Digby to Windsor, Nova Scotia. Through all the trials and tribulations I had kept my cool, but as the train seemed to crawl up the Annapolis Valley I began to have second thoughts. What am I doing? Will I know him? Will I like him? Will he like me? What if he isn't there to meet me? And then complete panic set in.

Even though I had fixed my hair and face several times, had given a quick brush to my uniform and buttons, now I huddled in my seat scared to death. My travelling companions were a naval officer and his wife and she, understanding lady that she was, spoke words of comfort and encouragement. Seeing that she was not getting anywhere with the mass of quivering nerves I had turned into, she took matters into her own hands. Ordering her husband to escort me to the door, she grabbed my suitcase and led the way. As the train stopped she put my suitcase on the platform and her husband very gently, but very forcibly, pushed me off the train. There was one solitary figure on the platform who was now running towards me. Well, the soldier and the CWAC have celebrated forty-three years of happiness, during which time life has been very good. We are now the proud heads of a family consisting of three daughters, a son and their spouses and six grandchildren.

When Jo Maxwell's husband went to war he was an extremely fit man:

We swam, dived, played tennis and won prizes for our dancing. He was a motorbike enthusiast, full of energy, very outgoing. He returned, repatriated from Germany, severely wounded. He had a head injury and suffered blackouts and, as his balance box was shattered, his balance was affected.

We had to change our life completely. He could no longer play games, dance, etc. It took a couple of years for him to be able to walk upright. He had to concentrate so much only to walk that it was impossible to go far afield. He tried to play golf but lost his

balance turning to swing; the same with fishing. We completely
changed our direction and, although we were told every year at his
medical examination that he would not live long, we had over forty
wonderful years together, both of us completely fulfilled.

*Kathleen Hasted was married in October 1939, when she was nineteen
and her husband was twenty-one. He was called up for the army in
January 1940.*

All I did was write to him and wait, wait, wait for the war to end.
Now the time passes so quickly, but then one week was like a
month. I got very independent during the war, having to fend for
myself and, of course, fight off young men who (some of them, not
all) thought servicemen's wives were easy game.

When my husband was demobbed in March 1946, I thought
what more could we want, but that was the start. You see, my
husband carried my image in his mind of me waving him off at the
station and six years later still expected me to be just the same,
dressed in the same clothes, etc. So it was a shock to him to find this
other independent person and, of course, grown up into a worldly-
wise (I thought then) woman. He, of course, went into the forces a
boy and came out a more than worldly-wise man.

It was difficult settling down. I'd lived life all that time as a single
woman and here I was pushed with – well, what can you say – he
was in some ways a stranger.

*In 1939 Elizabeth McGonigal was twenty-six and living in Glasgow
with her two children. Her husband was in the Royal Fleet Auxiliary,
stationed in the Indian Ocean:*

Time dragged on and after two years my husband was home. He
just appeared with no advance notice. We had a lovely reunion for
four weeks and then he was off again. This time the trip lasted one
year (without leave). My husband was discharged, 'unfit for further
sea service', in 1945.

Now the aftermath: attempting to hold a job at his trade as a
chef, he wasn't very successful. The years at sea during the war

caused him to have a breakdown. He was eventually admitted to hospital, where they gave him a prefrontal lobotomy, which was supposed to relieve his confusion. I wasn't aware this was an experimental operation and is no longer performed or I would not have consented. After three years in hospital I was allowed to have him home at weekends, when I wasn't at work. I learned I was six weeks pregnant and, at the time, was overjoyed, as I thought a baby would help Ed get better. However, at eight weeks the doctor informed me that my husband would probably never be wholly cured (he had deteriorated after the operation) and wouldn't likely be able to leave the care of the hospital. So, for the next three years I visited him daily until he died at age forty-three of heart failure. He never was aware that he had a small daughter who really missed having a dad. I never remarried.

Iris Tasker's husband had been overseas in the Royal Army Service Corps for four years:

I was a civil servant but, because I had no children to look after, I had to do compulsory Auxiliary Firewomen Service on the switchboard once every six days. Time went by and the war seemed eternal, and then there were rumours that the war was ending.

It was with terrific excitement that I was working in the office when a call came through for me. I answered and heard that one voice I had always wanted to hear for so long. It was George! He was home!

I sat down in a daze. The girls I was working with said, 'Go home!' They made my face up, combed my hair, put my coat on and I don't remember to this day how I got home! We grinned at each other like scalded cats and fell into each other's arms. No, I never ever let him down and could look him in the eyes with love and devotion.

We had two sons and they are a credit to him. Unfortunately, I lost my beloved in 1986, but we had lots of lovely times together. I'm an old woman now and a crock, but I was blessed with a good husband.

The end of the war brought some people problems they were unable to foresee. For Doreen Garrington the war had been particularly stressful and the peace did not put an end to her troubles:

At the beginning of 1942 my husband foolishly wanted a divorce. This I refused to do. Until he was posted, we lived in the same digs but had no communication, and it was a relief when he was posted to the West Indies, where I heard nothing from him for three and a half years.

The Americans were looking for suitable girl drivers at their various bases and I was fortunate enough to be selected, where I had many happy times and a multitude of friends. Later, as the war was coming to an end, I transferred to the US Air Force in Europe. I continued to work there but, for the first and last time in my life, I fell hopelessly in love, although I realised we were not suited in many ways. When V J Day arrived he was sent home to the States in the first batch and I requested leave to return to the UK.

Two days later I got an even bigger shock. My almost-ex-husband appeared. How he found out where I was living I shall never know. This was the most traumatic time of my life. He wanted to try to get together again. I felt fear and frustration, but no way could I resume any marital relations for many months.

My husband accepted an excellent post in India (he was a brilliant aeronautical engineer). I stuck the appalling climate out for nearly three years before being invalided home, complete with a young baby.

Dorothy Richards was married just five days before her husband left for France. He was away for five years and spent most of the war in Poland after being captured at Dunkirk:

I was living with my parents. It was quite a trying time. I worked in a café in the High Street. The girl from the post office brought a telegram up. It said, 'Arrived safely. See you soon.' I went up to his mother's and we waited and it was a day later that he came home. The local policeman came to the door and said, 'Have you seen who's coming up the road?' And he just walked up the road and that was it. He'd had to find his own way home. When I think of all the fuss that's made of them today when they came back it's utterly ridiculous.

He had changed a great deal, really. He'd lost a lot of weight and he was very, very difficult at first because he didn't want to do much. He wouldn't queue; he said he'd been queuing for years. It's psychological, I suppose. He wouldn't let me waste anything because he'd given up his watch and God knows what for food in the camp.

I was very happy to have him home and then you realise that you've not got the same man back. His mother, as well, couldn't understand how he'd changed and how difficult he was. He was ill, you see, and it took him two or three weeks to really come around and then he began to feel better. He still had a lot of the prisoner of war in him. Even now you can't touch his things. In the prison camp they only had a certain limited space and what was theirs was their own and nobody touched it. It's continued all his life and I have to be very, very careful. He wasn't like that at all before he left.

When he first got back he was bothered by waste and having to hang about for anything. He did go back to work for a time to his old job, but he had sudden blackouts. He couldn't become the manager of the butcher shop because he couldn't remember things. He managed to cope eventually but it took a long while, three or four years.

At first it was difficult to sleep with him again. In those days you didn't have relationships before marriage and we only had five days of marriage, so it was quite difficult. But that grew and was quite all right. We're very happy now. We had two boys and we've done very well, we think. We've got six wonderful grandchildren. We consider ourselves very lucky.

Charlotte Belfield's boyfriend was called into the army at the beginning of the war. They were married in June 1941 while he was on leave:

He came home from India on New Year's Day 1945, not knowing at all what he was going to do. The end result was a massive nervous breakdown.

It took £250 for a specialist and shock treatment at the hospital in Nottingham. It was a terrible experience – no putting you to sleep first. So, there was I, six and a half months pregnant with a very sick husband. He had seven more shocks and ended his working days as an electrician.

We had a lovely daughter after all that and now, at seventy-six, he is a pretty fit man, except for occasional bad memory lapses.

For some, married life had been short indeed. Gwen Eccles was married on 17 February 1940. Just thirty-six hours later her husbnd was gone:

He was posted missing in Norway on 17 May. From Norway they were taken to East Prussia and worked on a farm there. As the war neared its end, they had to set off and walk 1100 miles to Lüneburg Heath, where the Americans freed them.

When I received the telegram to say he was on his way home I knew that all my prayers had been answered. We would be together again. He arrived at Barrow Station about 5.30 p.m. on 11 May 1945. When I saw him leaning out of the carriage window my legs went like jelly and I shook all over. After all, I was twenty-one when he went away and five years, three months, is a long time. I thought we would be like strangers, as we had been parted longer than we had courted one another. Fortunately we just clung to one another as if it had been only yesterday. He always said we were the only couple married five years who had never had a wrong word.

Betty Hammond's husband was sent to the Middle East in 1942. The next time she saw him was in 1946:

We were determined to keep in touch as much as possible and I wrote two or three times a week and sent as many snapshots as we could, film being in short supply.

When I opened the door to him the evening he came home neither of us could speak. We laughed, we cried, we kissed, we cuddled, we just couldn't believe we were together again. It seemed so long since we had been able to touch each other. He was so handsome, so brown and so happy to be home with me. I thank God so often that he came home as good a man as he had left and for the many, many years of happiness we shared afterwards.

My husband died three years ago after being married for fifty-four years. The only time we were apart were the years he spent in the forces.

Ivy Harding's husband returned home in 1945 after being called up in June 1940. He served in the Gordons and then joined the Airborne Divison:

He called on his old employers while on demob leave. They were able to offer him a job at their Thameside Wharf, but to us this was a major catastrophe as it was so far away in Dockland and he had always walked to work, saving on any fares. So he borrowed a bike from an uncle. It was quite a sight to see Bob coming down Old Kent Road on this rusty old bike, proudly wearing his red beret (minus winged badge), whistling *The Ride of the Valkyries* as loud as possible, waking up the neighbours. He did well, though, ending up as transport manager and buying himself a car!

Bob told me that on the boat returning home in '45 with the parachute regiment, they were played records over the tannoy. As they neared Dover it was quite a sight to see, as six-foot paras were in tears as Dorothy Squires belted out *Coming Home*.

Marion Deviney (now Sherwin) waited for a young airman to come home from the war:

He was just nineteen when he left for overseas. It seemed too young to be married, though I was almost three years older. The day soon arrived when we had to say our goodbyes. His father and I drove him to the Cobourg, Ontario, railway station. I kept back the tears as my mother had said, 'Don't let him see you crying.' However, when I got back in the old Buick, I turned on the windshield wipers. They didn't clear up my problem. Then I remembered the sun was shining. It was tears, buckets of tears.

It was a lonely time, but as a schoolteacher I was busy. I looked forward to his blue airmail or little brown filmed letters and I wrote often.

When summer holidays came round in 1944 I went back home to the farm to help out my brother and my mother. Dad had died and they needed me.

It was the third week of August and it was hot — hot back on the flat where I was hoeing endless rows of potatoes. My little sister Ruth came back to bring me a drink of cold water. I began to wonder if there would be a letter from Gord. I hadn't had one for quite a while. It was so hot, I hardly dared ask her to walk to the village post office at Vernonville to pick up the mail, just in case. However, with the promise of some small change, she set off. An hour or so later she was back and, sure enough, in her hand were two small blue airmail letters, both from Gord.

I devoured them. They brought the best possible news. He had finished flying twenty-eight operations over enemy territory. Now flashed through my mind his very words: 'When I have finished my tour of operations and get my little gold wing, I will come back and marry you.'

Quickly I looked at the dates the letters had been written. Yes, he had plenty of time to have completed two more trips making the required thirty, and we hadn't any bad news, so by all means he had finished his tour and he would be home on leave — in all possibility. I was so relieved that he had survived, was safe, would be coming home with his little gold wing and we would be married.

To express my joy I began to scream and yell and finally to sing in my own raucous way my version of war songs: 'Oh, he's there in the air, in his flying machine, this someone I love.' And, instead of bell-bottom trousers, coat of navy blue, I love a sailor and he loves me too, I sang my own version: 'Small-bottom trousers, coat of air-force blue, I love an airman and he loves me too.' I sang out, the woods echoed and the dust flew along the endless rows of potatoes. I was very, very happy.

The next day the thresher moved in. It was Doug, Mom and I for it as Dad was no longer with us. So we got ready for the threshers, about a dozen men. We had placed basins, soap, water and towels outside. It was noon and they had gathered to wash up. Mom and I had things under control on the food front. The men came in, sat down at the table and pitched in. The phone rang. I answered.

It was Gord's mother. She never phoned me. Why was she phoning? Fear spread over me. She said, 'We got on of those nasty telegrams today. Gordon is missing in action.' Somehow I made it to the pantry. I stood behind the door, crying my heart out, oblivious of the ravenous threshers.

When I pulled myself together after the distressing news, I decided to go by bus to Cobourg to see Gord's parents. Perhaps some news would follow.

His mother was made of steel and she was in control. His dad was a very sentimental person, he wiped his eyes with a big white handkerchief. He was crushed. No news came. I felt useless hanging around. I went back to the farm. I was needed. I went robot-like about the endless farm chores.

I never doubted that Gord was dead. My mother would say perhaps he's all right somewhere. I thought, What does she know of the dangers he faced? Some of my girlfriends had similar experiences of their boyfriends being missing in action overseas. They continued to write letters, thinking they were alive some place and would some day receive their letters. They were never heard from again. That wasn't the route for me. He was dead and I knew it — there were no more letters to write.

When I wasn't working in the fields I went to my room and lay on the bed. I cried, I rolled and tossed. When I began to scream I buried my head in the pillow. To keep from threshing about, I clenched the iron spindles of my bed. Nothing was working. I got up, I went downstairs and turned on the radio. The announcer said, 'And now we will play the popular new song, *Lili Marlene*, as our troops sing it, as the Germans sing it and as it will be sung in victory.' I was immediately alert as Gord had mentioned that song in his letter. He had said, 'I like the song *Lili Marlene*. Do you know it? We got it from the Jerries.' 'Underneath the lamp post by the cottage gate, My darling, I remember, that's where you would wait.'

It was his song and it was being played now as it would be played in victory. Did it mean something? No, if only he weren't missing and could come home and we could both hear it in victory together.

Nonsense! He was never coming home. I walked to the village. Perhaps there would be another letter that he wrote before he died.

'Hello, Marion. Have you heard from Gordon? He's alive, I know it.' This came from a little American girl visiting in the village. 'I'm saying my rosary,' she went on.

It was sweet, but she was only a little girl. She had no idea what war was like.

There was no letter from Gord but there was a sympathy letter. A sympathy letter! My God! That was more like it, though. Yes, she, too, knew that Gord was dead and she was sorry. Thanks.

Sunday would definitely be a hard day, more time to think.

'Please, Marion, come to church with us.'

'I can't.'

'We don't want to leave you alone. You'll see friends.'

I went along, but I couldn't face going into church. I waited in the car and thought how many times I had prayed for Gord in that church and how we planned to be married there. Well, God had not heard my prayers.

We arrived home and I was about to go up to my room when the telephone rang. I answered. A voice said, 'This is a cablegram for Miss Marion Deviney.'

'Speaking,' I said.

'Back in England. Feeling fine. Love, Gordon.' We had a foster brother in the R C A F overseas, too. I knew he had been injured in a crash and until the very last word I thought it was from him. But they had said Gordon. Was it Gord, back in England, feeling fine? I was confused. Could it really be Gord back in England? Gord safe, feeling fine?

The phone rang again. It was Mr Sherwin. 'Gordon's safe,' he said. 'He's back in England.'

Then I knew for sure. I hung up the phone and ran outside to tell the others. 'Gordon is safe! He's safe! He's back in England. He's feeling fine! He's not dead! He's safe!' I collapsed in my mother's arms.

Again, I thought I should go to Cobourg to rejoice with his parents. My brother drove me to the bus. I saw a friend on the bus. 'Gord's safe,' I cried, 'safe in England.' There were squeals of joy as she grabbed me and hugged me and she told a friend and that friend told someone else and soon the whole busload was rejoicing that one girl's airman was safe.

Not long after this was another cablegram, phoned out from Cobourg. It said, 'Coming home soon.' With this wonderful news the house seemed confining. I began walking outside across the lawn, through the little orchard, across the rye field, into the wood field, up the hill to the highest spot on the farm, a very suitable spot for a mountain-peak experience. I turned my face to the sky. It was caressed by soft breezes. The ordeal was over. I thanked God for saving Gord's life and I asked Him to forgive me for having so little faith.

Well, Gord did come home that October. He phoned me at my boarding place in Peterborough and asked me to meet the bus at the Empress Hotel that evening. It was all so wonderful. I later learned that some of my pupils had learned about the reunion and had come to watch, but all my thoughts were on his homecoming. The bus stopped, people were getting off and there was an airman and he came straight to me and took me in his arms.

We didn't get married right away. The war was still going on and he would likely have to go back. Well, the war ended over there in the spring and in the Pacific in late summer. Now he faced becoming a civilian and finding work. I hoped he would go to university but he had a love affair with trucks, bought a small licence and went to work. We were married in 1946 and we are still in the trucking business – milk transport – forty-four years later.

It's another story, his story of being shot down over enemy territory, of being befriended and hidden by a French family.

Thirty-three years later we discovered the French farmhouse abandoned. We left a note, just in case. We were soon to receive a letter from an old lady, eighty-two years old, who said, 'I am so glad to know that you got back alive.' We looked at the signature. It was only then that we learned the name of the family who had sheltered Gord – the Morgand family.

Forty-four years later our son Jay and his wife Jane met Georgette Le Boulch, daughter of that French family. Georgette and Peter took them to the family farm where Gord had been sheltered after parachuting to earth from a burning plane. They showed him the field where Gord had parachuted to earth, the barn where he was taken in by the Frenchman, the house and the attic where he hid from the Germans and the cellar where they all sought shelter when the battle raged over the village. They sent back his parachute harness.

Now, forty-six years later, Gordon and I will be in Switzerland to

64

visit our daughter, Dr Elizabeth Sherwin, and we will go to Paris and we will see Georgette Morgand. Though she doesn't speak English and we don't speak French, it will be a profound moment.

It was not easy being a loyal and devoted wife in wartime Britain. Many husbands and wives barely knew each other before they parted, and the regular letters back and forth could not always counteract the constant temptations and need for companionship. Although living conditions were drab and stark, there were still places where it was possible to escape for a few hours – and they were full of the uniforms of overseas armies.

One woman had to say goodbye to her husband when he was sent to North Africa. He was away for five years. A friend tells the story:

Well, of course, during that time so many marriages broke down – there were so many American, Polish and French soldiers over here – but actually it was an English soldier, an officer, who she fell in love with and he said he would marry her. So she wrote to her husband down in Africa and said could she have a divorce, she wanted to marry someone else.

And then she discovered that this officer had moved off to some new location without leaving any address or anything. His mates told her that he was already married anyway. She had already written to her husband asking for a divorce, but actually they did get together again afterwards. There was a bit of acrimony between them over it, of course. I think it took a lot of tolerance on his part.

Jean Kingsman was a child at the time, but she still remembers the surprise that met the next door neighbour's husband, Mr Dixon, when he arrived home from the Far East:

Mrs Dixon had been made pregnant by a black Yank. I saw her the day after her husband returned. She had a black eye and later had a miscarriage. Her husband wouldn't let her outside the house for years after. She was great friends with my mother and I remember them sitting around the kitchen fire discussing different ways of abortion – gin, hot baths etc.

My father knocked on our window when he returned from Italy, and Mother's Irish boyfriend disappeared out the back door. We never saw him again.

Later, out walking with my father, he confided in me that Mum was pregnant by another man. I gave his arm a hug. It didn't make any impression on me because we were already a large family – a baby every two years – so one more didn't make a lot of difference.

Vivian Fisher was married in 1942 at the age of seventeen:

My husband was in the RAF and unfortunately the forces proved too much for him and he went absent without leave about six months after getting married. I did not hear from him, but I heard from the regimental police that he had deserted and was known to be going to undesirable houses. I did not know what to do and then my mother suggested that I should start going out to dances, etc., which I did.

I met a man, John, who was in the REs, serving as a batman to an officer who was stationed where I lived. As time went on we fell in love and consequently I had a baby girl, Victoria. We were both thrilled at the birth. In the meantime I had put in for a divorce from my husband. The baby was only seven months old when John wrote to say he had been sent to Oxford and decided to marry someone else. I was devastated, as was my family. It took me a time to get over the hurt. Then one day I went out with my baby Victoria and my sister to a park, where we met two American Airborne officers.

One of the officers immediately fell for me and I for him and we started a beautiful friendship. I told him all about my life but that didn't deter him. He was goodness itself. He said he would marry me as soon as I got a divorce. I then found I was pregnant again by him. I told him and he made me an allowance for myself and the forthcoming baby. He was then posted to Holland and I did not think I'd see him again. But one day after my baby boy, Graham, was born, I arrived home to find him back from Holland. He adored his son and preparations were made for me to go to America with both my children.

Then one day a knock came at the door and who should be standing there but my husband Cliff. We talked and talked. He immediately took to both my girl and boy and acted as if nothing had happened. He told me that he had returned to his unit and then been posted to India. He had written to me and then torn up the letters because he didn't think I'd ever want him again. In the end we decided to try to make a go of the marriage again. I wrote to the USA to explain to Jimmy, who really took it like the gentleman he was.

The end of the story is that my husband and I remained married for forty-four years, had three other children and were happy until he died in September, 1985. He was both blind and without legs, but I loved him.

After many years of letter writing the opportunity to speak left many tongue-tied. Phyllis Hopkinson's husband had been a Desert Rat with Monty for four and a half years:

After this period I knew he was on the list for coming home and was not surprised when the phone went one day and it was my husband ringing me in England. Our conversation went rather like this: 'Hello, Muriel, how are you?' A moment or two went by before I could reply and I said to him, 'Oh, Charles, I am fine. How are you?' In other words, neither of us could think of anything else to say.

He duly arrived at our house and our little girl, who was just four years old by then, came down the stairs and saw this huge man in uniform, promptly burst into tears and wet her knickers! However, the day passed, although somewhat strained and trying to get used to the idea of a man again around the house.

That night I was awakened by a smell of smoke and thought the house was on fire, so hurriedly put on the light. There was no husband by my side, just a lot of puffs of smoke coming from the floor on the other side of the bed. When I looked over there was Charles, lying on the floor, smoking his pipe. He informed me he could not sleep on a mattress after so many years away. At the time it all seemed very strange, but I am glad to say we had another little girl about a year later and had a very happy marriage until he died in 1976.

Valerie Jones (née Simmons) knows how difficult it was for her mother, Ethel:

Whilst my father was in the army, my mother met a Canadian soldier who was stationed near where we lived. They became very close and, but for the fact that she was already married, they would probably have been married. But, as she often says, she had made vows with my father in church and she had to keep them. Not only that, but she had me, at the time about four years old. So, she sent her Canadian back to Canada.

My father came home and there we all were. I didn't even know him, he was a stranger to me. As I grew up my mum would often talk about the Canadian. As my mother became older and my father became ill I thought how wonderful it would be if I could find my mum's Canadian. Not much chance – no address, the other side of the world, forty-three years later. But I found him in Ontario. My mother could hardly believe it. She rang him up and they talk to each other regularly on the phone. My father has now died and my mum's Canadian is divorced from his wife. My dearest wish is that they should meet again.

For many, like Mrs Freeman, the first few years after the war were worse than the six years they had lived in the thick of it, on the east coast of England:

When my husband went overseas I was a young girl in my early twenties with a new six-week-old baby. My home became a pile of rubble two weeks later. I had to grow up quickly.

So, when the time came for my six-year-old to meet this strange man, she asked him, 'Are you my Daddy?' All the anticipated joy flew out of the window a few hours later with a sadly distressed little girl wanting to go home to my sister's home and five children.

This strange, dark man was telling me how different it would be when he took over. We had no home, no money. Yes, it was a hard time but eventually we all adjusted, but no way were we the same as we were in 1939.

When Jill Hopkins's father went off to war as a major in the Royal Engineers, her parents' relationship was already strained:

My father did not return until 1946, staying in Holland with the forces of occupation, involved as an engineer in the rebuilding of bridges, etc. His last letter to us, long since destroyed, was shown to me, an awkward, insecure, nervous eleven-year-old, by a shattered, devastated mother, whose world had come to an end, like so many of her contemporaries who had bravely struggled on through enormous difficulties and hardships. In the letter, he briefly told her of his love for a young French girl and that he wanted a divorce, for which he would provide ample evidence of adultery.

My father married his French girl in 1948. She was then twenty, a few years older than me. Maybe as a result of injuries received on the battlefields of northern France or the second marriage that wasn't as happy as he had expected or maybe as a result of so much battle or emotional conflict, he took his own life in 1966. He left two grieving widows. After his death, my mother became a chronic invalid. She never ceased to talk about him, sometimes with affection but mostly with a hatred born of sheer misery.

Vera Raby's marriage was never the same after her husband returned from the war:

We were married in 1943, after a parting of more than two years, during which time my then fiancé was serving on HMS *Eurybus* in the Mediterranean. Before he joined up we were very close, and talked endlessly on anything and everything. After our marriage I was able to join him in rooms in Glasgow for eight months while his ship was in dry dock. I thought we were very happy. Upon leaving Glasgow, I returned to my village home, and eventually had a baby boy, but my husband was sent to Australia and only saw the baby briefly once. While in Australia he lived in one hotel, worked in another, was befriended by Australian families and generally enjoyed life, which was good after his time in the 'Med'.

The war ended, and he came home in January 1946. I was thrilled at the thought of life together at last. My parents gave up part of their house so that we could have our own sitting room, kitchen, front door, staircase and bedroom. I begged clothing coupons to get a new dress, and went to meet him at the local station on a cold dark February evening.

He hardly talked to me, he didn't appear to notice anything about our little 'flat', or that I had tried to 'dress up' and prepare a little meal. The next morning he was annoyed that Paul, aged nearly one year, cried at the sight of a stranger in 'Mummy's' bed, and seemed to lose all interest in him, and everything else. I found out that his parents had met him the night before at Banbury Station, to tell him they had arranged for him to join the staff of his uncle's village school in Dorset, prior to going to Weymouth Teacher Training College the next year. To my horror we were on our way four days later, still not talking or communicating about anything.

He got on well with his uncle, in school, and out of school activities, so much so that I saw very little of him. Sex was very infrequent, and I began to think something was wrong with me. Eventually I was so unhappy I went back home, until he'd finished his teacher training, but to this day (and now we are both seventy) we do not talk or communicate except in a quite desultory way.

I could never understand why he should change so much between sailing off to Australia, and ten months later his return, demobbed. Maybe today, with various kinds of help and counselling I could have coped, and perhaps found the person I fell in love with, so many years ago. We have two sons and a daughter, so life hasn't been all bad, but the closeness and affection never came back.

Gwendolyn Boles and her boyfriend had married after knowing each other only three months:

He had pawned his watch to buy my wedding ring and a silver heart-shaped locket.

On 4 February 1946, one year and one day after our marriage, my husband, whom I hardly knew, came home. I can only remember how thin he was and he trembled from head to foot as he hugged me. He was probably as frightened of the future with this person with whom he had only spent a few weekends as I was.

We had to get to know each other, but we were young – twenty-two and twenty-three – and we grew together. Everyone seemed to be living to give the boys some happiness, something to come back to and some stability.

Clara Clewlow had been married for two and a half years when her husband, aged twenty-eight, was sent overseas. They had two children. He was away for nearly five years:

I was living in Kingsville – a small town near Windsor, the most southerly town in Canada – when my husband came back. He was coming by bus from London, Ontario. I didn't have a phone in my apartment at that time. The phone call came to my mother and she eventually got the message to me through a neighbour that he was to come on the bus on this certain day. I met every bus that came from London to Kingsville that day and there were about four or five. The last one to come in was around eleven o'clock at night, so I got a neighbour to stay with the children. I'd taken them with me to the bus station every other time during the day. They were four and six years old. The little one, the four-year-old, had never known her father.

Anyway I got a neighbour to come in and stay with them, so I went up and met this last bus and some friends and neighbours came with me to give me a little moral support. Here we were waiting and the first bus came in and stopped and some people got off, but no Arthur Clewlow. The bus driver said, 'Don't worry, Madam, there's another bus coming behind.' So we waited. The second bus came in and stopped and some more people got off, but not my husband. He said, 'Don't worry, Madam, there's a third bus coming.' I was just about in tears by that time. Anyway, finally the third bus came and he was on it. He was thinner than when he left; he was a bag of bones.

In many ways it was very difficult for him to adjust. He couldn't sleep in the bed, for one thing, he'd been sleeping on the ground for so long. I'd got a new bed and mattress and a whole new bedroom suite and he couldn't sleep on it. Night after night he got out of bed and lay on the floor.

I couldn't believe that our son remembered his father because he was only two years old when he left, but the boy and his father got off right off the bat very well. But this little girl who had been born after he had joined the army and was only three months old when he went overseas treated him as if he were an interloper; he didn't have any right to be there. It was difficult. Before my husband came back we had a neighbour who had all sons and loved my little girl and loved to make a fuss over her, but she wouldn't let him touch her because there was no man in our house.

My brother used to come and visit and she wouldn't let him touch her either.

I think I tried to be too firm with the kids and my husband was inclined, of course, to be very soft when he returned. I realise now that I probably went to an extreme to overcome what I thought was his lack of discipline. My daughter was a teenager before she finally became accustomed to her father. It took close to ten years.

We had no problems getting back together sexually. I have to say we had a marvellous sexual relationship all our married life, extremely satisfying to both of us. You wouldn't believe the letters I've received since his death last year. People have said that just being with us made them feel good because they could see the love that was between us. We were married fifty-two years, with three children, five grandchildren and one great-grandchild.

5

'Look, kids, it's Daddy'

*T*HE HOSTILITIES WERE *over, but for many a period of new suffering was about to begin. For the women of Britain who had survived horrors unknown in previous conflicts, it was a time of expectation. Unlike the wives and mothers throughout history who had waited in the safety of their homes for news of their loved ones, women had faced an enemy who brought havoc and destruction into their living rooms. They had suffered pain and dangers that could be compared to the experiences of those serving in uniform. World War II had been fought not only on the field of battle, but within the home itself.*

To the women who had shouldered the pains of wartime parenthood, it must have seemed that their role in the victory received little acclaim. Now they were faced with a further difficulty – sharing their responsibilities with a partner many of the children hardly knew. The occasional visitor on leave who arrived with presents and left after a few days was a far cry from a permanent, resident father. How would the children react to a stranger in the house? Who was this man and what part would he now play in their lives?

It had been a hard war for Doll Talbot. With her one-year-old son in her arms, she had said goodbye to her husband Howard before he left for the Middle East in 1939. One lunchtime she returned to her tenement building, only to be handed a 'We regret to inform you' telegram, telling her that her husband was missing and believed killed in action.

Months later the joyous news arrived from the Red Cross telling her that he had been seen in an Italian prisoner-of-war camp. The official word came soon after: he had been captured at Tobruk. For this young mother the long years of waiting were about to come to an end. Her husband had been released by the Russians and was on his way home. Her son, Howard Junior, now almost six, knew his father only from photos and because of his nightly prayers that God would take care of him and bring him back. Doll remembers:

I had just got a flat near the Elephant and Castle. Howard came home by cab. It was completely unexpected. I was putting new curtains up at the time. Young Howard was in school. It was very difficult for him, as they were strangers, complete strangers. In fact he was scared of him at first, more or less.

Like most children at that time, I don't think he ever did get over it, not really. The point is that the first five years of a child's life are the most important. I was fortunate in having a husband like I did. He didn't insist on taking over and was wonderful.

What made it hard was the fact that he had been treated so badly as a prisoner; he'd lost a tremendous amount of weight. He was home just about a year when it was found that the malnutrition he had suffered in the camp had caused him to contract tuberculosis and he was sent to hospital for five years.

It wasn't so much the air-raids and what we had been through, but I think it was feeling that now it was all over and we could look forward to a new future. But finding that you can't, you don't know what's in front of you, now that my husband was in hospital. But, of course, the advantage was that unlike the prison camp, I could see him. The years after the war were tough, but they were tough for a lot of people, not only us. You see, it didn't end. Not when the Armistice came. That's when the troubles started.

Those men who had attained a rank that accustomed them to giving orders had an air of authority about them. This could be intimidating, especially to children.

Rosanna Blyth's husband volunteered for service just two weeks after war broke out and was gone one week after that:

My little girl was then four years old and I was angry that my husband had no need to go but chose to leave us instead of staying in an important job and protecting us. He quickly rose to the rank of CSM 1 and was posted overseas, ending up in Burma, so it was six years before we saw him again.

When he came back home our little girl was ten and didn't know who this overpowering man in uniform was and he, of course, didn't know her. He still thought he was in command of men and treated us like army personnel, spitting out orders that must be obeyed and, consequently, we became quite afraid of him and all the aggression within him.

It really had a devastating effect on our lives, as my little girl and I had been so close because of all the trauma of bombing, air-raid shelters, etc. We both resented this man who dominated our otherwise close and loving relationship. It did something to all of us so that we were never able to get back on the same level as each other ever again.

Those six years apart certainly took their toll. My husband, being a man's man, missed all his army pals and all the power his command gave him and resented very much having to be an ordinary civilian again. We, on the other hand, were equally resentful because our own close relationship had been disrupted. So it didn't make for a very happy time for many years, or ever again, if I am honest.

Pam Rendell (now Wood) had been evacuated and was brought back home when her father returned from being a prisoner of war:

The next day, as a special treat for my homecoming, my mother asked me what I would like for tea. I was completely unaware of shortages, as there was an American base near the hospital and they had spoiled us children completely with sweets, toys, ice-cream and fruit. My particular favourite at that time was bananas and ice-cream and that was what I asked for. My poor mother must have scoured the whole of Somerset, for there at teatime was one banana. My sisters had never seen anything like it and were most suspicious of it. I had always been a very finicky eater and proceeded to pick away at this banana.

My poor father had, of course, not eaten anything like a banana for many years. Eventually he could stand the strain no longer and said, 'Pam, look at that pretty bird outside.' I immediately went to the window to see the bird and, yes, when I came back to the table the banana was gone! I decided that I did not care too much for this strange man who pinched my banana.

Like most families, we settled down to pick up the threads of normal family life. My father's health had suffered through his years of internment. A six-footer, he came home weighing just over eight stone and was soon diagnosed as tubercular. He had lost all his teeth and felt the cold terribly. He was luckier than some in that he soon got a job as a laundry-van driver, but money was very tight. Holidays were unknown. The two weeks in the summer that my father had off were spent working on a nearby farm. My father helped cut the corn, my mother joined the other women stooking and we children were expected to make ourselves useful, helping with the stooking and taking the food and cider to the men. There was a bonus when the men reached the centre of the field. All the animals in the field had collected there and the men would take their shotguns to them as they bolted out of the corn. This meant that we would have rabbit to eat for the next few days.

The other side of the coin was that accidents were all too common and my father had the misfortune to fall off a hayrick, breaking both his ankles. I think it was at that point that the tension between my parents came to the surface. My mother had been used to being in charge of the household and finances for many years and did not take kindly to having a man about. She had been a nurse in London and then joined the land army, putting my sisters into nurseries, and she had become very independent. My father had come back home expecting the situation to be very much the same as when he had left.

During the war years my mother appeared to have had a very good social life, going to the pictures and dances or just down to the pub, and she had no intention of giving this up just because my father was home. He was looking for a nice, quiet life with a once-a-week night out with the boys and did not take kindly to Mother's gadding about. Very soon they were fighting, which led to each going their own way and leading their own lives. Inevitably they split up and we four children (another sister was born in 1947) were taken away and put into children's homes. My mother had a severe illness ending up in a psychiatric hospital and my father disappeared from our lives.

Although I had such a short time with my father and we had started off so badly with the banana episode, we became very close and I was devastated when he left. But there is a happy ending to this rather sad saga. Forty years later I went back to Somerset and, through a series of coincidences, I found my father. He was dying in a nursing home, but we had the most wonderful reunion.

I asked him about the war but, like many men who had served in the war, he was quite reluctant to talk about it. Even after all those years he was very bitter about the way he was treated after the war and he had refused to accept his medals. He had been a professional soldier before the war. He in fact served a total of twenty-four years in the army, but, because of the break in the middle, when he married my mother, he did not receive a pension of any sort and no compensation for the fact that his health had been ruined by his internment. Add to that the breakdown of his marriage and the loss of his children, it is not surprising that he was bitter about the war and his subsequent treatment.

Nevertheless, he was still the lovely man that I remembered as a child. Three weeks after we were reunited he died, but he had waited for me to find him, for which I shall always be grateful.

When my mother recovered from her illness she was homeless. In order to get us girls back she had to find somewhere to live. We were eventually housed in a Nissen hut on an old army camp just outside Chatham. It was awful – boiling hot in summer and bitterly cold in winter. Although there was a bath in the hut, there was no hot water. We had to put a shilling in the meter in the bath-house in the centre of the camp and then bucket it back to our hut. Naturally, it was nearly cold by the time it got to our bath, so we did not have too many hot baths. There were only two bedrooms in the hut, so we four girls had to share a bed in one of them while my mother, stepfather and baby brother had the other one. The living room was a tiny, dark room with one small window high up in the corner and off it was a slit of a room, laughingly called the kitchen. My mother lived there for several years until she was eventually rehoused in one of the post-war council estates which are now little more than slums. Because of the appalling living conditions in the hut, we girls were again taken away and put into children's homes and there we remained until we left school.

So, you can see the war really destroyed our family, not in the way that so many families were destroyed, by death and destruction, but by the strain that was put on two ordinary people who just could not take it.

Joan Pender (now Wardrope)'s parents also found it difficult when her father returned. She had only been seven when he went into the army. He was away for over five years, and for half of that time he was a prisoner of war.

My dad lied to get into the army because they wouldn't have accepted him with five children. My mother was 'Rosie the Riveter' and worked at De Havilland.

My dad was only five feet one inch. He was one of the smallest soldiers; in fact, he was never able to get boots to fit him, he always wore boys' sizes. He was an unemployed musician, which was why he joined the army.

But I remember him coming home. We all went down to meet him. Mum dressed us all up and we all had to stick together and look for the smallest little soldier. Everything was wonderful that first day. Then the drinking started. I was the only one, being seven when he went away, who could remember Dad the way he was. The war changed him. And what I still remember was him butting cigarettes out on the floor like he was still in the prison camp. He was just a completely different person to what he was. It was terribly hard for Mum. Then Mum had three more children. So it was like two families.

Mum finally left him when she was sixty-five. He died three months later and was buried on 11 November, Armistice Day.

For the children of the war, fathers were figures brought to life by mothers' stories and faded photographs. The constant reminder that he would soon be home built up an image of a white knight who would gallop over the hill and, with a wave of a magic sword, make the world a place of love and beauty. The fairy story all too often fell far short of reality.

In spite of her father's absence, Bernadette Bennett had enjoyed a very happy wartime childhood:

As an only child, my relationship with my mother became very close. I was constantly reminded that Daddy loved me and would be home after the war and we would be very happy. But when he did eventually arrive home, it was a very different story.

In the first place, it came as a great shock when he arrived unexpectedly at the front door one night. Subconsciously, I mustn't have expected him ever to return, but here he was and he looked massive to me (he was six feet tall). His voice was terribly loud, as he was a gunner and was used to shouting above gunfire. He was so overcome with joy at being reunited with my mother that I was just left on one side for what seemed like ages. I felt so forlorn, a little eight-year-old girl watching someone else take over the mother who had been all mine for so many years.

I always felt resentful towards him for coming back and spoiling what had seemed to be such an idyllic mother-daughter relationship. I know he always regretted being absent during those very crucial formative years of my life and he tried to overcompensate by being very possessive, to the extent that he discouraged my friendships. He was also very, very strict and, to an extent, I was, for want of a better word, frightened of him.

Those who were too young to remember their fathers leaving were, in some cases, fortunate. Although she was a small baby at the outbreak of the war, Beryl Darlison points out that she never felt shortchanged during those difficult times:

As 'war babies' we, as a group, have always been considered deprived, but I find that a difficult observation to agree with. You don't miss what you've never had and I was surrounded by a large family of bombed-out relatives squashed into a semi-detached house. It was fun and exciting for us children. We were unaware of the strains and stresses. We had the thrill of seeing and touching a banana and understood the shortages of bread and eggs.

With thousands of servicemen returning home, it was only natural that there would be mistakes. Marshall Litherland was a boy at the end of

79

the war and had returned to Liverpool from being evacuated to North Wales:

All the servicemen began returning from the war at this time and each was welcomed home with banners and flags draped across the street and around the house where he lived.

Now, this particular night was Friday and I remember it because Friday night in our household was always bath night. We brought the tin bath in from the back yard and placed it on the mat in front of the fire. We then took it in turns to have a bath. My mother was always last to bathe and all us kids had to sit out on the stairs in the lobby to afford her some privacy.

On this particular night there came a loud knock on the door and my mother shouted from the living room, 'Who is that at the door?' When I went to inquire, a voice from the other side of the door said, 'It is your dad, home from the war.' When I told my mother, who was still naked in the bath, she panicked and shouted, 'Tell him to go away.' So I went back to the door and told him to go away, whereupon the letter-box opened and two eyes peered in and saw me behind the door and my three sisters sitting petrified on the stairs. The letter-box closed and we heard footsteps disappearing up the street.

I have often thought of the ecstatic welcome the soldier must have expected, to be coming home from the war to meet his wife and children whom he had been longing to see for the past four years, only to be told to go away.

On the following day a soldier knocked on the door and I opened it. He apologised profusely for knocking on the door the previous evening and frightening us all. He'd got the right number all right but, in the dark and in his excitement at getting home, he'd come down the wrong street. He explained that he realised that he was at the wrong house when he looked through the letter-box and saw all the kids sitting on the stairs for, as he explained, he'd only got one when he left to go abroad some years earlier.

It's impossible to imagine how strange it must have been to a child who had been born after its father had left for overseas duty. Lorna Penry-Davey introduced her husband to her son:

My husband left for India a month before our son was born and returned when the boy was two years old. His first meeting with his father was a formal handshake and 'Good morning.' Our elder son David, at the age of seven, was watching a firework display and became very agitated, as he thought the war had started again.

Although the future Mrs Barbara Crowder was only two and a half years old, she clearly remembers the day her father came home to Canada in March 1946. There was quite a group. Her mother, grandfather, Aunt Blanche, Aunt Mary and Great-aunt Eunice all gathered in the crowd at the Canadian National Exhibition grounds in Toronto, waiting for the arrival of Corporal Ralph W. Ibbotson:

The surrounding crowd seems pretty misty now, but I vividly recall looking out at the sea of uniforms from my vantage point in my mother's arms. There were hundreds of soldiers, lots of noise and I suspect that I must have picked up the anticipation and excitement of the day.

Suddenly, way across the building, I saw a man raise a tan leather suitcase up on his shoulder. We had sent him a leather case identical to the one I'd spotted, so I studied the man from this great distance and yelled out, 'I see him, I see him! I see my daddy!'

As my father walked towards us in the waiting area, my mother rushed towards him with me in her arms and they embraced and kissed. (In retrospect, oh, how important it was that she included me in this intimate reunion.) I said, 'Me too. Kiss me too,' and I recall the first hint of the stranger's face near mine, his little prickly moustache scratching my skin.

When we were seated in the back of the big, black car with a driver and on our way home, my new dad asked me, 'Would you like this apple?' bringing a huge, red apple towards my hand. 'No, thank you,' I said, feeling very shy and a little nervous. 'I have something else for you,' he said, smiling, and showed me a bright and shiny silver coin. 'I'm not allowed to take money from strangers,' I replied quickly. He paused and looked down at me and said, 'I'm not a stranger. I'm your daddy.'

I could tell I'd said something really wrong. This was the first time I recall feeling embarrassment and shame. It was a tense moment, and a harbinger of a future strain between us.

The rest of 1946 was filled with many moments of crying and misunderstanding both for my dad and for me, and lots of negotiating. The bonding process was painful, filled with out-and-out hostility on both sides at times. My father would slap me at the table for not eating all my food 'when children were starving in Europe'. I told him to 'go back where he came from' after a row in my sandbox. I decided, at one point, I didn't like this interloper. My mother was constantly in the middle, trying to be shared by both of us. It couldn't have been an easy time for her.

On the day that Dorothy Foster went to meet her husband, her little girl was ill and had to be left at home. Dorothy remembers that it was extremely hard for them all when he returned:

He'd changed and I'd changed. We'd grown up, let's face it. I was very young when I got married, just seventeen and he was twenty-four. He'd had it rough, he was all through Germany, Holland and Belgium. I think one of the toughest things was for my daughter to get accustomed to having him around. For one thing, she didn't like uniforms. And it was very hard for her and very hard for him. I lived with my mother and my mother had spoiled her and there had been no man around the house at all for all those years.

And I'm telling you it took all of three or four years before it was nice to have him home, I'll be honest with you, because he had changed so much. He was used to the discipline. He was a sergeant-major and thought he was going to be the same in the house and I was determined that he wasn't going to be. We were almost in the middle of World War III in no time. You know, when you've had the child by yourself and somebody thinks they're going to start telling her what to do and everything, it's pretty rough. Unfortunately she ran to my mother all the time more than me. She was a grandma's girl.

Well, I'll tell you what had happened. We had had one child, a baby. She had to have an operation and she'd died. So it was very rough. He had known the first one when he left. She was almost a year old.

The trouble was he expected to be waited on and everything was done his way, so it was hard for him, too. And if there was any man that spoke to me he would have it that I'd been out with them and all this kind of stuff. I think they figured that all we ever did back home was run around while they were away. Anyone that knew my mother would have known that that was impossible. But to tell you the truth, I never even thought about it. It was difficult as well, sexually, because you just sort of felt used, more or less.

Janet Flemming-Kunc grew up near Manchester:

I clearly remember when my daddy came home. I was around seven years old and in the middle of cleaning out the shoe cupboard. My rear half had just backed out of the cupboard when the door knocker sounded with a smart rat-a-tat-tat.

'Mum,' I called upstairs. 'There is somebody at the front door.'

'Answer it, love,' came the reply. 'I can't come now.'

Threading my way through the variety of footwear, I went to open the door. Standing on the front step was a man in khaki uniform, a kit-bag by his side. Before he had time to speak I said in my best grown-up voice, 'Please wait. Mummy will be down in a moment.'

I had been told many times over by friends and neighbours that 'Your daddy is away winning the war' or 'Your daddy will be home soon now, love.' I don't know why I never made the connection between this soldier and the return of my father.

I had gone back to my shoe sorting, paying no attention to the soldier. Mother came downstairs and all I remember after that was the word Daddy and being squeezed so hard I could hardly breathe. Rough khaki, like sandpaper, scraped away at my face and a hard brass button was pressing against my ear.

My neatly laid-out footwear was pushed aside and the big kit-bag deposited in the middle of the kitchen floor. Delving into it with cries of, 'Let's see where Daddy has put the choc choc for his little Janet pal.' As much as I wanted the chocolate, I was not prepared for this.

Who was this person to march in and spoil my work, talk to me like a baby and expect me to sit on his knee and call him Daddy pal? My daddy would never behave like that. Why, I was practically grown up. Who was this insensitive stranger who had disrupted our morning with his rudeness? It never got any better.

I had so looked forward to the return of this prince amongst men. For one thing it meant a week off school, to get reacquainted, they said. In my case it was not getting reacquainted, it was plain getting to know the person who, up till now, I only knew through myths and built-up images.

The reality was a far cry from the sepia photographs. Sure, he had the medals and probably deserved them, but to a seven-year-old the medals were only pieces of metal stuck on striped ribbons. Try as I might I could not step back in time and become the two-year-old again.

Mother went back to working in the mill and I came home to a cold, empty house. She had less time for me now and talked more to 'him' than to me. 'He' would march in my little bedroom, where I retreated more and more, to see if anybody was fishing in the canal, rearranging my little treasures on the window-sill as he opened the window to get a better view. I was outraged and vowed to tell my mum. From this dubious start the situation escalated into open warfare. By the time I was ten or eleven we were simply not speaking.

My mother, who, as she put it, was left to fend on her own, got no credit. She was the one who worried about the blackout curtains or having to wrap her child at the sound of the sirens and hurry down into the Anderson shelter in the middle of the night. She was the one who saw me through all the childhood illnesses, sat up all night when I was delirious with fever, while trying to manage on meagre rations.

According to him that was nothing compared to life in the trenches. 'At least you got treated like a hero,' she would throw back. My mother, who had learned to cope, resented the return of this chauvinistic warrior who tried to take over – especially since he could not manage his way out of a paper bag, since the army had done all his thinking for him.

The battles raged on. The seven-year-old was bewildered – this is not how it was supposed to be. Gone were the cosy times with Mum, to be replaced by a military regime. This sergeant stole the mum I knew, changed our life and expected to be hero-worshipped for it. I feared and hated this new person in our lives and yet somewhere in this child's brain was a feeling of guilt. I knew I was supposed to love and respect my father who had been fighting for his country.

'You brought her up' and 'Well, it was your choice to join up and leave us' were sentences I was to grow familiar with as they were constantly thrown at each other. I felt like a ping-pong ball between them. Ping: 'Here, you try raising her.' Pong: 'You taught her to hate me.' Back and forth, back and forth I would hear them. At night in the sanctuary of my room I would pull the covers tightly over my head and bite the back of my hand in order not to cry. As the rows got worse and I was dragged more and more into their private war, I started to do badly in school. My only escape was to retreat into a world of fantasy.

My sole desire was to get out of that house. Obviously it was my fault these two people did not get along. More than anything I wanted to be part of a family, a proper family. At eighteen I left and came to Canada. At nineteen I married a young man who had a wonderful, welcoming family; at twenty-one I was divorced. Next, I was engaged to another young man who had an even bigger, wonderful, welcoming family. After four years the relationship came to an end. Several years later I remarried a kindred spirit: a European with no family whatsoever.

In 1988 my father died and my mother followed him eighteen months later. It is ironic that as my mother's ashes were laid next to my father's in the field of honour, the last words said over them by a Legion member were, 'There, now they can quarrel all they want in peace.'

I realise as an adult that really my father was not the sole bad guy. My mother perhaps should have taught me to respect him no matter how she herself felt. Neither of my parents were really to blame; they were victims of circumstances, as I was myself. I do blame the war and sometimes still feel bitter about the invisible handicap I have.

When people expressed sympathy for my children having no father, I often felt, yes, but it could have been worse; they could have had one like mine.

'Look, kids, it's Daddy'

Sheila Scott's father was a soldier long before the war began. By the time he was married, he was already a sergeant-major. He was offered a commission after the Battle of Arnhem, but refused:

It would have been necessary for him to stay in Berlin with the occupation forces and my mother flatly refused to move to Germany or even into army quarters in England. Consequently he left the army and came home in the late autumn of 1946. Up to that time I had not really been aware of him – he had been a stranger who occasionally appeared overnight in our house and then disappeared again after a couple of days or so. Most of the time I was actually afraid of him, especially if he perched me up on his shoulder when he had on his peaked cap. I didn't like the way it covered his eyes and made him look down his nose at everyone.

When he came home for good, I found it very difficult to adjust to having this brusque male presence in the house the whole time. I had grown up for seven years with only women – my mother, the other young mothers in our street and for two years my grandmother lived with us.

I didn't like the way my dad ran our home like an army barracks. At the time I wasn't able to talk to anyone about my feelings, and my mother didn't tell me anything about her feelings until much later. But apparently he resented me for preventing him (as he saw it) from pursuing his army career! He believed it was because of me that Mum wouldn't go to Germany and, of course, he never forgave me for not being a boy!

Not knowing any of this, I endured a miserable existence for twelve years. It seemed to me that no matter what I wanted, needed or asked, Dad always said no. He ruled me, Mum and my sister (who was born in 1947) with a rod of iron. I never had a key – I always had to be home by 10 p.m. – and, when I wanted to go to college to study graphic design, I had to leave school. He found me a job (office junior) and I had to bring home my wage packet (unopened) and give it to him every Friday.

Mum didn't say much, but it was not a very big house and I couldn't help overhearing the frequent quarrels. He drank more and more as the years went by. By the mid '50s it was quite usual for him to disappear on a drinking binge for the entire weekend.

My sister and I had to pass inspection every morning before school (shoes polished, teeth brushed, neck scrubbed and bag packed just so). We could not go out anywhere after school (only Saturdays). We never went anywhere as a family – we didn't even visit other relatives and no one ever came to our house. We were not encouraged to have friends, let alone bring them home.

By the summer of 1959, I had had enough and I just walked out. I went home to see Mum once a week (when he wasn't there) until she died in 1964. After that I didn't see him again until my son was born in December 1968. Even so, our contact from then on was only the usual ritual of birthdays, Christmas and my sister's wedding. He only ever came to my house once.

It may seem a terrible thing to say, but I wasn't really very sorry when he died in July 1989. Although I do regret that we didn't have a better relationship. I feel sure that the war had something to do with it and I have no doubt that thousands of other people my age have experienced something similiar. I feel sure that if he hadn't had to go away to war then we would have been much better friends.

There were no men left in Pat Lord (now Grant)'s house once her father had gone overseas in December 1939. He came back in February 1946:

I kind of remembered him, but it's hard to know whether I remembered it or people told me.

I was going to be ten that year, 1946, and I was sick and tired of everyone else's dad coming home and where was ours? And so I told my mother if he didn't come home for my birthday, he didn't have to bother, and she wrote and told him that. Now I don't know how my stand influenced him. My birthday was 3 March. He was in Britain helping get the other fellows home; he was a sergeant.

We were living in Fergus, Ontario. There was a telegram or something that came to my mother that said she should meet him in London, Ontario. We stayed with my aunt and uncle, who were just like a mother and father to us, anyway. I remember I was in grade six and I was so stunned; I was so excited. I think my sister and I found seventy-five cents and we bought one of those great big signs that said 'Welcome Home, Daddy'. Now, we never thought how we were going to put it up and here are these two kids at noon hour and

I remember this man, Mr MacLean, came and put it up for us right across the door.

My dad got home about four in the morning and I'll never forget it. My sister and I had our chenille housecoats on, we couldn't sleep, we were so excited he was coming home. This man walked in, not with the army hat we'd seen him in – he had the beret instead of the side cap – and he'd taken his moustache off. We went into the foyer of my aunt and uncle's house. He came and we just stood there. He looked at us and we looked at him and he seemed ten feet tall. My mother said, 'Go hug your father or something.' So we went over and he knelt down and hugged us. The dog was afraid of him.

We went home to our own home and we sat around the table. He brought us gifts – matching dresses – but, of course, my mother had bought them.

The four of us sat around as a family for the first time ever.

Sometimes we forgot him after he got back. We'd be writing to my aunt and uncle and I remember my mother saying, 'Don't forget to mention your dad.'

He was out of the army but he didn't have any other clothes to wear except army clothes for a while. We moved to St Thomas, Ontario, and he went back to a railroad job.

My sister and I got very good at playing the ends against the middle in about two weeks because my father couldn't say no to us. I think it drove Mother nuts. He was a really liberated man and he treated us as people, not girls. So we didn't have in our home female/ male roles – I think because there had only been the three of us before, so whoever had the boots took the garbage out. This continued when my dad was home. I don't remember any friction between my mother and dad.

I was just getting into a rather individual stage of my life. I remember I didn't come home once when I was supposed to and both of them were very annoyed with me. I said some smart remark and my father flipped me right over his knee and gave me a couple of pats on the bottom. I was indignant; I was so angry. I was told to go up to my bedroom until I felt like coming down and apologising. I never came down that night.

My dad died two years after he came back, from shrapnel in the spine. He died at home with the three of us with him, on his birthday. It was very hard and I was very angry at God for quite a few years.

Janet Day-Williams lived with her mother and her father's parents in a Victorian terraced house in the centre of Leicester:

My dad was away at war and everyone used to say, 'When your dad comes home this . . .' and 'When your dad comes home that . . .' and I suppose I must have looked forward to that day with some trepidation.

Anyway, as promised, a strange-looking thin man turned up at our doorstep (where I used to sit) laden with presents for everyone and loving my mother. I got a rag doll, which I would have treasured to this day except my mother threw it away, and a leather Indian-style handbag.

I can honestly say that from that day until last June (at the confrontation) the relationship with my father and my mother had been quite tragic. I always knew that they both loved me, but whenever I was with them both I always felt 'in the way'. When I grew up and married the first time at the age of twenty it was to get away from this feeling. The man I married was a similar war child and he felt the same about his parents, and although we weren't really suited, this drew us together.

Whenever I went to visit my parents after this I felt the same, and when I left them I felt lonely and desolate.

Anyway, back to last June. I confronted them about my feelings, saying that I knew it went back to wartime. I reduced my mother to tears and my father was very quiet. Imagine having to be told for the first time at forty-seven years old that your parents did actually want and love you and that it was the war that messed everything up! I was born on 22 October 1942. My dad had left for India and Burma three weeks before and was in Durban, South Africa, when he heard the news of my birth.

Soon after I was born, my mother began to work in a factory that had been taken over for the manufacture of munitions. So for the first three and a half years of my life I was mainly looked after by my grandparents. I'm sure they treated me very well, but apparently not so my mother, who was totally miserable and missing my father whom she then (and now) doted upon. Consequently, my time with my mother, when we could get to be on our own, was a very close and loving time. When my father arrived back on the scene, she always seemed to be afraid of showing her love for me and, of course, he found it very difficult to love me.

What I'm trying to tell you is that I loved and adored them both; but that the repercussions of the war can last for forty to fifty years. All this is no fault of theirs or mine.

The perfect time for a return was when everyone was in the house and lined up beside the door, waiting for it to open. But with children at school it was not always possible to arrange this.

Geordie McPhee was two years old when his father joined the Royal Artillery and went to Burma. He returned one day in 1946, just before Geordie arrived home from school for lunch:

I knew my father was there even before I saw him. He was sitting to one side of the fireplace on a small seat. He must have been expecting me to rush to him, throw my arms around his neck and we would become bosom buddies immediately. What happened was quite the opposite. I resented him coming into our house because I felt he would make changes.

We never really bridged the gap in our relationship until he had a severe stroke, which left him paralysed down his right side without his speech. The strange thing is that we were able to communicate *then*, sometimes even without words.

Terry Palmer (now Andrews) was playing in the street, as usual, when a soldier came walking down the street with a kit-bag on his back:

He was spotted by a playmate. I heard someone say that perhaps it was my dad.

This man came closer and closer and I remember we all stood like statues, watching. The next thing I knew this face was bent down, looking into mine, this strange face I thought I'd never seen before. To a young girl of eight, it was a bit alarming. As he looked down at me, he said, 'Do you know who I am?' I looked at him and thought, No, not really. But I remembered someone saying it must be my dad, so I said to him, 'Yes, you are Mr Palmer.' I couldn't bring myself to say 'Dad' because I had never called anyone Dad, or not that I could remember, and I certainly didn't know this man at all.

I remember that for a long time after, I always called him 'Mr Palmer'. I did eventually learn to call him Dad, even though it never seemed right and didn't sound right somehow. He always felt like a stranger, more like an intruder that had come and taken over my life and my mother's house.

I remember my mother saying that the war had turned him into a very serious person. Things my sister and I did were never right. We just couldn't seem to do right for doing wrong. There was always this stranger finding fault. I remember saying to my mother once, 'Why does he keep moaning so much?' She replied, 'He used to laugh a lot once.'

The war changed the course of our three lives because it changed my father so much.

Kitty Molloy was eighteen when her husband was called up in 1940, supposedly for six months. He served for six years:

He just saw our daughter, who was born in 1942, then his regiment was shipped abroad in July 1942. He was finally demobbed in January 1946. Our daughter was over three years old when he next saw her and she didn't want to know 'that man', as she called him. Naturally, he was terribly upset about it.

Linda Crust's father was a Methodist minister. They lived in a manse and, with his departure for the war, lost their home as he was no longer the resident minister. Linda was three years old:

My mother, my older sister and I spent the next six years roaming round England imposing ourselves on friends and relations. In 1942 my sister went to boarding school so, apart from school holidays, I lived with my mother acting as a single parent.

During the war years I saw my father only three times. My father had escaped from Dunkirk, but no one in the house knew of this. I was in bed with my mother when we were wakened by a man entering the room. I remember the shadow of a soldier holding a torch standing by the door. My mother screamed. I was bundled out of bed and suddenly the landing was full of cousins in nightclothes shouting out, 'It's Uncle Fred.' I didn't recognise the soldier, who was my father, but I was pleased and excited with the others. I spent the rest of the night in bed with cousin Betty and my sister.

The last leave my father had came when we were living in a boarding house in Southport. I was thrilled to have my father near at hand. My mother had always tried to build up a favourable image of him throughout the years he was absent. Every Christmas and birthday I had received a book with the words 'To Linda with love from Daddy' written on the title page. Because of these presents I never doubted that my father loved me and thought of me. When I was about seven it did occur to me that the handwriting in the books was not the atrocious, spiky, angled writing in which my father's letters to my mother were written. It was some years later before I realised that the handwriting in the books was my mother's writing.

My parents wrote to each other every single day throughout the war. My mother received my father's letters in bundles, perhaps some weeks apart. I remember her crying with frustration once when my father's terrible writing defeated even her experienced eye and she failed to decipher a letter. The letters travelled round with us throughout the war. By the time my father was demobbed in 1945, there were two suitcases full of his letters. Shortly before she died in 1958, my mother asked my sister to burn these letters without reading them, which she did.

My mother did have one bonus from our time in Southport. Women were required to work in the statistics branch of the civil service, which operated from a hotel on the sea-front. My mother applied for part-time work and was accepted. She was delighted by this and even more delighted when she discovered an unknown talent for maths. She never had other paid employment during her married life.

When my father finally came home, we were living in Leicester. Our dream was to come true of a family life together. I was wildly excited and demanded a ride on my father's shoulders as soon as he came home, although I was by then a large nine-year-old.

Like many fantasies of heaven, our family life fell short of our expectations. My father found it difficult to settle down to such a different way of life. My mother was jealous; she was also a nagger. My sister was shy and adolescent and I was clinging with both parents. Family life was a terrible disappointment to us all, I think. I was argumentative and my father was irritated by my dreadful vowels. For years we had all nursed an idyll in our minds and reality was hard to bear.

Almost fifty years on, the scars inflicted at the end of World War II still affect some who were children then. When a strange parent re-entered the home, the children often felt they were being pushed to one side. The pain, although it might have been hidden, could scar a child for life. Although this man was known as Daddy, his demands interfered with the comfortable setting to which a child had become accustomed. A bed was more than just a place to lay a head. It was a haven for many children who snuggled against their mother for comfort during the bombing.

Once Daddy returned, this haven was no longer available, as Catherine from Manchester found out. She was born in 1943, while her father was away in West Africa, and her mother took her to live with her aunt:

When everyone started saying to me, 'Your daddy's coming home for good soon,' I didn't really understand what a daddy was. I just hoped it was the man who had the khaki overcoat and not the strict man always correcting me who had the blue overcoat.

I slept with Mum but, as the war came to a close and Dad came home, of course I went back into my cot. That feeling of rejection and resentment stayed with me and when my own husband, a regular soldier, was away I never took my babies into bed with me.

Throughout my life I could never do anything right for my dad and it was only the last fourteen years that we really got on. Sadly, he died just over a year ago. Mum died fifteen years ago and could never watch war films or anything to do with the war on TV, so great was the effect of the war on her.

I do feel never knowing Dad until I was two and a half was sad for him and me and I expect there are many more like me.

Another girl, who was older than me, went with her mum to the station to greet her dad at the train when he came home. Her mum said, 'There's your dad.' She saw two soldiers coming towards her and ran to one, saying, 'I'll have this one for my dad.' Of course, it was her dad's mate. Her dad never forgave her and she was only four years old at the time.

The Red Cross came to see Maureen Curtis's mother before her husband's return, to warn her what to expect. He had been a prisoner near Munich during the war:

They told her that some people accepted capture, others didn't. My father was one who didn't and she would probably find him a changed man. They hadn't been married very long and were both only in their early twenties.

When my father returned, he couldn't talk about what had happened to him and would spend days staring at the wall, unable to speak. These days he would have had counselling, of course. My mother didn't know how to cope with him and he would fly into violent rages for nothing. At sixteen years old I couldn't understand why I was still suffering for the war.

The Germans had smashed both his kneecaps and run a bayonet from ear to ear round his throat. He arrived home on walking-sticks and I am told I screamed the place down, which made for a difficult relationship. He was obsessively possessive and insanely jealous of any boyfriend I ever had. He was also an adulterer. Unfortunately he died of cancer in 1976.

Many young soldiers were deeply scarred by experiencing the horrors of war at close hand; they needed love and understanding.

Sarah Patterson's father suffered from nervous strain after the war. Life for her and her mother changed radically when he returned.

I saw my mother defeated and dejected, for the first and last time. Not that she did not have cause to be again and again, but she must have drawn on some inner reserves to keep her strong.

My father had been on active service for almost five years, in a branch of the army that had brought him into great danger, and he had been awarded several medals. He would never talk about his experiences. Shell shock and a battered nervous system were not always recognised then and he had obviously appeared to be perfectly physically sound when he was discharged. But his nerves were actually at the breaking point – and he made my life a misery.

After the quiet and placid life with Mother, it was a terrible change. I am not sure if I was a naturally timid child, but I certainly developed into one. To some extent I am still fairly retiring and I find new situations, people and places quite an ordeal.

However, I believe that my sister Lizzie, born about a year after my father returned home, suffered even more. She eventually developed a stutter. Mealtimes with him were a nightmare, as he picked on us both for the slightest transgression. I suspect that my poor mother became very unhappy and that she, too, was near to a breakdown.

Even though I am now aware of the reasons for my father's behaviour – his occasional violence and almost permanent bad temper – it does not lessen the impact it had on our family at the time. My relationship with my father did not improve. If anything, it became worse. Even my mother did not seem to understand me. Perhaps it was just my father's attitude – still very difficult and quite cruel at times – which prevented her from being more sympathetic to me.

It was not easy to overcome the problems facing the reunited families. Children had concocted a dream world, the centre of which was the man that Mum said would soon be home.

Most families, like Hilda Day's, persevered and eventually built a new life. But it was a painful process:

I was married in 1939 and said goodbye to my husband before he went away until 1942. He came home on a week's leave and left me pregnant. He didn't come home again until 1946, a stranger.

I'd been on my own all that time, made my own decisions and brought up a child, and home came a stranger to us. Our daughter didn't know her father. She cried, so he lost interest in her, except to tell her off when she did wrong, so she'd turn to me. He sulked when I made a decision. It was a long time before I could let go. He didn't like the rationed food we had and accused me of having an affair with his brother. He wouldn't believe I'd been true to him all the years he'd been away. I loved him, but I was so unhappy.

We spent an uncomfortable time together until I became pregnant again. He still wouldn't accept his daughter and by that time she wanted him. One day I made him listen to me and we talked about how things were. He said he wasn't used to married life and, although he loved me, he'd rather have stayed in the army. But he said he'd try to settle. He was sorry about his treatment of his daughter, but he hadn't seen her grow up and it didn't feel like she belonged to him. He did try to change. It took quite a while but, after his second daughter was born, he was the man I knew. Today, after illnesses, no money at times and all the things that can either make or break a marriage, we are in our fifty-second year and still very happy.

Val Cowley lived with her mother and elder sister on her grand-mother's farm in Dorset. Her father was in the army and had been posted abroad in November 1940; he didn't return until Val was five:

So, as you can imagine, when this strange man came home and started trying to tell me what to do I really resented him. To make it even worse, my mother had a much-wanted son.

I can remember the first outing in a car with my father. I just opened the car door and fell out. When we went to Fortes in Bournemouth to have tea, I had ice cream and got the spoon stuck between my front teeth.

Dad used to have very black moods which, as an adult, I can now understand. He had been a prisoner of war and had been lined up to be shot four times.

On the day war broke out Evelyn Hale said goodbye to her husband and didn't see him again until June 1945. He had been taken prisoner in Greece. Their little boy was only eleven months old when his father went away:

On 1 June 1945, we were so excited receiving a telegram from my husband to say he was coming home. Around 5 p.m. a knock came on the front door. He didn't use the knocker, only his hand, so I thought it was my son's little friends calling him out to play. I said to him, 'Go and tell them you can't come out till later on.'

He went to the door and then walked up the hall, looked at me and said, 'It's a soldier, Mummy, with a kit-bag. I think it's your husband.'

Oh, dear, I could cry now when I think about it. Well, my husband and I just stood in the doorway, holding each other and crying.

My son, I think, regarded his father as an intruder in our lives. One day he said to his grandfather, 'Is Mummy sure that man is her husband, 'cause he doesn't talk like us, does he?' He was a Wiltshire man.

Blanche Bunkle's husband received his call-up papers in 1941 and left to join the Royal Artillery Coast Defence. She had two sons, one aged two and a half and one five. It was not easy for either of the boys when a 'new' man moved into the house at the end of the war.

The younger boy couldn't remember his dad in Civvy Street and, when he was demobbed five years later, he resented his father checking him if he misbehaved. He said, 'Mum tells us what to do,' and 'When are you going away again?'

Robert Appell will not forget his return easily. He had been wounded in the final days of the conflict and had returned home to Canada on a hospital ship:

It was a beautiful day in Halifax when we arrived and on the dock a forty-piece band played *Sentimental Journey*. Many moist eyes around.

Mine was a belly wound and I had an open colostomy, so the train trip to London, Ontario, was uncomfortable. I was carried on a stretcher from the train. Twelve people were there to welcome me, including my twenty-month-old son, whom they plopped down on my abdomen. Well, I winced, the boy cried and then we all laughed and embraced.

It was hard for sons and daughters, who had been first in line for their mother's affection, to stand to one side as the returning husband occupied the limelight. It was just as difficult for fathers to watch a child they had dreamed of holding for so many years turn away and reach for its mother.

Kathleen Rennles was married in 1941. Her husband left for service overseas and did not come back for four and a half years.

I had a baby daughter . . . Janet was three when he came back and, of course, she didn't really want to know her daddy, did she? If anything went wrong she wouldn't go to him, she'd come to me.

It was great to have him home but, of course, he wasn't the same as when he went away because of all those years away from us. He'd lost pals as well and so I think all of them were like that. When they sat down to relax you could see their thoughts were far away.

He was wonderful with his baby daughter. He wanted to do things for her, whereas she didn't want to know. It was only natural because she'd been with me all that time. But she came to know that this was her daddy. For me, it had been a lonely life without him, I will admit that.

It was all very strange when the war finished. You didn't really believe the war had finished. You were still on tenterhooks, do you know what I mean? We'd had all those years of war and it took a lot of settling down after that. Rationing went on for quite a long time after the war had ended. We were literally rationed to every degree. But, I say, you have to make do and mend, and where you couldn't get fresh eggs you had dried eggs. I've queued many a morning just to get two eggs for my baby, Janet. We used to walk miles to get those two eggs for Janet. And bananas, we used to have to queue for them. You never got very many sweets. Perhaps that was a good thing.

Pat Whitby and her husband were married in December 1940. She was pregnant when he left in March 1941, to serve in Iraq. He had been there for nearly four years when she got the word that he was coming back:

The day arrived when he was at last home. The first few weeks he was at home were fine. My little boy was quite happy with Daddy. He could pick him out of the photos my husband had sent. He eventually went back to camp for demob.

When we were all living together permanently it was very difficult. My husband, I think, didn't contemplate coming back to me as a woman with a four-year-old son. He had left behind a young girl with no responsibilities.

He also felt he was playing second fiddle to his son and, by the same token, my child felt he was being pushed out by this stranger, so I was getting tantrums from him which I had never had before. I sometimes felt at the end of my tether and shed many tears, especially when I had waited so long and had thought when he came home we would be one happy family.

However, we did eventually settle down but, to my regret, there was never the closeness between him and my son that I would have liked. We never had any more children. My husband died nearly two years ago and, even up till then, there was still a barrier between the both of them. My son, although quite a good son, is an introvert. I sometimes wonder if his early childhood had something to do with it.

For wartime children, the world was largely populated by women, who filled many roles their men had vacated. Schools and stores were mostly staffed by women, and women became the head of their household. For girls without brothers, the transition to having a male at home could be difficult. Jean Dyson was born in 1937 and was an only child:

My father was called up into the army. He was sent abroad to India and Burma, where he spent the remainder of the war. During the time he was away he wrote regularly to both my mother and me, taking care to print my letters so that I could read them myself once I was able. I thought the world of him and thought Mum a poor second! If she had cause to reprimand me or, worse, smack me, I would always say, 'I will tell my dad what you have done when he comes home!'

Once we had news that he was definitely on his way home, we were all excited. He returned during the evening and I was called from bed with the good news that he had arrived. I can still remember the long walk from the bedroom down the stairs, every step bringing me nearer to having to face my father and what I would do if my worst fears were realised and he was a black man! I

99

had seen regular photos of him but I was still very worried. The relief was tremendous.

I can't remember how I treated him after this, although Mum said I treated him as a stranger. Coming home from school with requests, Dad would give his permission but I would ignore him and go to Mum. This caused Dad a great deal of unhappiness.

Sylvia Gable's father went overseas during the war when she was four years old. She remembers that when her mother told her and her elder sister their father was coming home, it meant nothing to her:

. . . because I didn't know who he was. I just remember that he wasn't there and then he was there. His hair had gone white and he had thickened out.

Because there was just my sister, my mother and myself we didn't really know any men. It was just that there was this different person who acted differently to what I understood adults behaved. At school they were practically all women as well.

There were always wars between my sister and him after a while, because she was so used to having her own way.

Patricia Grafton's father volunteered for the Royal Air Force and was away for long periods of time:

Inevitably, during his service my mother and I were very close (I was, at that time, an only child). My father, whom I loved, became a hero figure, no doubt reinforced by media propaganda and fervent patriotism at the time.

The family became female-oriented, the male members — uncles, cousins, father — were all in one or other of the armed forces.

I used to took forward to Father's leave. As I grew older, there was a slight change in my attitude, an anxiety and unease when he returned. Life was interrupted and my routine altered.

When he was demobilised on 5 November (a few sparklers available) there followed ambivalence, although not recognised as such, and resentment on occasions. For so long my mother and I had shared life. She had been sole guide and mentor. Suddenly there were two people deciding what I may or may not do. Also, my mother's undivided attention turned from me to my father, causing some resentment. This situation, fortunately, did not last. I do not know if my parents were even aware of my feelings.

As the male members of the family returned, the picture changed again. Aunts resumed housewife roles and my mother returned to domesticity.

In 1941, when Jean Sparks was eleven years old, the eldest of four girls, her father was taken prisoner in Crete. He spent the remaining four years as a POW in Graz, Austria:

Being the eldest, my mother depended on me a great deal; consequently I grew up very fast. I left school at fourteen years and had been working over a year when the war ended and felt myself to be a grown-up young woman. (How I cringe when one thinks back.) However, things were very strict in those days and Mother and I had numerous battles over the wearing of make-up. Her constant cry was, 'When your father comes home he will not let you do this or that.'

I was at work when the longed-for day arrived, with no prior notice. Mother rang to say Father was home. When I got there, the house was full of family and friends. Of course, he did not really recognise any of us girls. Mother told him who I was and the very first words I spoke to him after all those years were, 'You need not tell me to take the make-up off, because I won't.' He never did, but the memory still fills me with shame.

It took us girls a long time to come to terms with having a man in the house, especially the youngest who, for many months, cried when he spoke to her. But we all came to know him as a very caring father.

When Irene Burke's father's ship docked on VJ Day, she felt sure they would be a complete family once more. Unfortunately it was not as simple as that:

He had last seen me as a twelve-year-old schoolgirl. I was now a precocious adult, fifteen years old, who had been standing in for him for the past three years as my mother's close companion and I wasn't to be easily relegated. In those post-war years, the troublesome teens when one is just an in-between had yet to be recognised and sadly we clashed at every turn and our relationship was never to recover.

When I finally married we were scarcely speaking to each other and it was my grandfather who gave me away. My father wasn't even there – by mutual consent.

Sadly my father died in 1967 when he was only fifty-seven. I had presented him with five grandchildren by then and we were conversing in a fashion, but we were never to be close and I will always feel it was another casualty of the war.

Shirley Chowne had a shock when out with her mother:

One day my mother and I were going into my grandad's café and she turned to me and said, 'When we get inside I want you to go up to that man and give him a big hug and a kiss and say hello, because that man is your daddy. He has come home.' I would not go up to him but stood behind my mother while this man took bars of chocolate out of his kit-bag and gave them to me. I gladly took them, I might add.

This was the end of the war and I did not like this strange man who was there all the time, having my mum's attention. One day I climbed on his lap and looked up at him and said, 'Do you think you will be going back to Egypt in a parachute?' With that my hand went up to his face, just missed his eye and drew five lines of blood down his cheek. This must have hurt my father inwardly so much, but to me, this man was an intruder and I did not like him there with me and my mother. It took a long time after that for me to accept this man as my father.

At the beginning of the war Sheila Yarrow's father joined the Royal Engineers. He left for the Far East and did not return for five years:

I was three and a half years old when the war started and nine years old when it ended. During his absence my mother and he wrote to each other, of course, and exchanged photographs. These undoubtedly helped both sides to keep track of changes in physical appearance. But for these, Dad would have had no idea what to expect when he came home.

This did not, however, cover the father/daughter relationship of knowing each other as people. Dad used to send me special cards – 'To Sheila, with lots of love from Daddy' – and I have a photograph of him in tropical uniform with a similar inscription on the back. Thus he tried to keep in touch with me, but, of course, the sad fact is that he went overseas leaving a virtual baby and came back to a grown child of nine years old – a large slice to lose of a child's life.

The day he came home is as clear to me now, forty-five years on, as if it were yesterday. We had known, to within a little, when to expect him. As the train on which he would travel passed the end of our garden, we would wait five minutes after each half-hourly train went through and then go to the front door to see if he were coming up the road. The inevitable happened, of course – he arrived late in the evening when I was in bed!

Now comes the part which stays with me so vividly and, as I write, makes me feel stressed. I am, by nature, a shy person, not given to much show of emotion, but I knew with certainty that, on this occasion, I had to act my heart out. I heard my mother greet Dad at the door and I heard him ask for me. He came to the foot of the stairs and called me. I steeled myself to virtually throw myself downstairs and hug him so that he shouldn't feel unwanted.

I know that he and I never grew really close in the succeeding years. He was a very amiable, good-natured man and we got on quite well – he, too, was of a quiet disposition and not given to bursts of emotion – but I always felt a constraint with him. My great sadness is that he died at the age of fifty-two years when I was twenty-nine. I feel that in my more mature years I could have got to know him properly. However my father was a gentleman in every sense of the word. How I wish we hadn't missed those vital years together.

Some children never missed their father; they had grown accustomed to being in the house without him. Betty Tymon (now Rostron)'s mother worked in a munitions factory during the war, while her dad served overseas with the British Eighth Army:

Mother worked to support us children. My brother Freddie and I had few memories of our dad and, in fact, never missed him. In 1943 Dad was in the Middle East when Freddie, aged seven, died.

I was ten years old in 1945. One Saturday, before Mother was due home from work, I noticed a taxi in front of the house. A soldier got out with his kit-bag and walked up the garden path. Taught never to open the door to strangers, I immediately checked the doors, making sure they were locked. I ignored the constant knocking, hoping he would go away. Eventually the neighbours came to assure him he had the correct address and that Betty was home. They called through the letter-box to persuade me that this stranger was my dad.

I didn't believe a word of it and said so. But I reluctantly let him in, on condition he stand inside the back door. Meanwhile, I had the front door wide open, intending to rush out screaming blue murder if he ventured one step further.

I viewed with suspicion the offer of Turkish delight inside the kit-bag and his attempts to jog memories of our family in the old house. But I was amazed that he knew so much.

Only when Mother walked in did I believe he was my dad. While they were embracing, I tore into that kit-bag, ignoring the souvenirs, parachute silk, Gurkha sword, Egyptian necklaces, Jerusalem bracelet and Indian shawls until I found that precious, rare Turkish delight.

Holding on to their precious pre-war photographs of loved ones, many women were shocked to see the physical changes that war had brought. Hair had turned grey or thinned out; bodies had become emaciated; scars had altered appearances.

What a photograph could not deliver was sound, and it was the surprise of her father's voice that Eileen Kerrow remembers:

I can relate to the end of the war as a child. My father was serving 'somewhere overseas'. He was absent for almost four years so, apart from a photograph of him on our mantelpiece, I couldn't really remember him.

However, with great excitement the day arrived for my father's homecoming. As his taxi drew up outside our gate, my mother was overcome with shyness and an attack of nerves and promptly ran and hid herself behind the kitchen door, leaving me to welcome my father!

As he walked up the path and greeted me, Father seemed much nicer and more handsome than his photograph. I was fascinated with his voice – it was so deep. Mother came out coyly from behind the door and, after much tears, laughter and much chattering, we enjoyed being a family again. It was many days before I would let my daddy out of my sight because I was such a proud nine-year-old.

My father died eleven years ago. He was a wonderful, kind man. The memories of him and those times will never fade.

Maureen King (now Merrett)'s father was a prisoner of war for five years:

At home, my mother was left with three children – me, my sister and my brother, who was born whilst Dad was missing. He was five years old when my father first met him. He had seen him grow up by photographs and through letters. Each night, after saying our prayers (in which we prayed for 'Daddy to come home soon, quick'), we kissed a photograph of Dad goodnight.

We had a very loving and caring family – aunts, uncles and especially our paternal grandparents. The highlight of each month was putting things together in a Red Cross parcel to go to Dad. Our grandparents saved their sweets coupons and sent bars of chocolate. Mum sent boots, underclothes, socks which she had knitted, toothpaste, shaving equipment, etc.

I vividly remember that day Dad came home. We were dressed in our Sunday best, my brother in his pram. We walked to Cheltenham Station, getting there far too early. My father had been a policeman and Mum was met at the station by a plainclothes policeman friend, who took charge of us children while Mum went on to the platform to meet Dad. I can see him coming toward us now – a tall man in uniform, with a kit-bag over his shoulder and an arm around Mum. What joy for me who remembered him. My sister and brother were rather bemused at this man from the photograph we kissed each night who was there in the flesh.

I think we took a taxi home and, in our absence, neighbours had put 'Welcome Home' signs and bunting at the house. My beloved grandmother was there.

It must have been traumatic for us as children, having to share Mum with someone, but we were at last a family again. Sadly, Mum and Dad have passed on now, but they are together again.

Although many homecomings were not as full of wonderment as children had imagined, at least they had the excitement of the moment. Those whose daddies did not return suffered the feelings of loss all over again when others welcomed their fathers at the door.

Christina McCarron-Pink was a child living in Liverpool when her father died of an illness while training for duty in Scotland. The highest paid job her mother could find was cleaning troop and hospital ships. Sometimes she was away from her children for two days at a time. It was a very difficult period for Christina:

I saw all my friends' fathers coming home from the war, but mine didn't. I remember one friend's father came home and after I saw him he grabbed hold of me and kissed me and he said, 'I'm awful sorry.' I was only eleven years old and I just felt, How come me? When he kissed me I just pushed him away, but it wasn't his fault he came home and my father didn't. Kids don't realise that, do they? I felt sad that my friends' fathers came back to their mums, and my mum and my brother, we had nobody come back to us.

We were burned out just after my father died – it was all in the same year. We had nowhere to live and people ran away with our furniture and rations. You wouldn't believe it. We used to live in a big house before we were burned out and we ended up in an up-and-down flat, but that's all my mother could afford. Because my father had died they wouldn't give her a war pension.

During that night the victory was announced the bells started to go. We woke up and everybody went into the streets and they were all dancing and everything. My brother and I ended up with friends or relatives in the centre of Liverpool. We were singing the songs of the war. At that moment, we never gave it a thought that our father wouldn't be coming back, because everyone was so happy that the war was all over. It wasn't until the excitement died down that you came back to earth and reality. I thought to myself, Hey, we're back to reality. There's all these men coming home and where's my father?

I called my brother my second father because he was the one who looked after me. He became the head of the house when he was only nine years old and suddenly had a seven-year-old to look after. I just took it in my stride because there was nothing I could do about it. My mother told us we had to look after ourselves and nobody else would, and you get kind of hardened to it. Today I'm a very pleasant person, but I won't let anybody step on me. These things kind of stick with you, you know. And I make sure nobody steps on my family.

I felt bitterness, not so much about the war, but about Hitler. I think I blame him as the individual that took my father away, that upset my life. Another thing I was quite mad about was that I was quite clever in school and we had to sit for scholarships when we were eleven. Well, the nun of our school wouldn't let me sit for it because she said my mother wouldn't be able to keep me in the clothes that were required for the High School, the uniforms and things would be too much of a burden on my mother. I resented that. I thought to myself that nun had no right to decide my future.

Barbara Mortimer was three and a half and her baby brother just eighteen months when a telegram arrived informing them that their father was missing:

I was brought up with photos of him. I worshipped him. 'Lost,' they said, and as the years went by we were brought up believing he'd come home.

I remember seeing a man in uniform at the top of the street. I was six then. I ran in shouting to my mum that Dad's coming. Then when I went back out, followed by my mum and her friends, the street was empty.

My mother was great. She joined in the street parties, dressing up as a clown, blacking her face. I was Britannia, my brothers an ATS girl and a fairy. The banners were stretched across the street. 'Welcome Home, Bill.' Then another and another, but never Don, my dad. I never spoke about it to anyone – but the pain inside!

When I was fifteen working at GA in Croydon, a letter came. It was the confirmation that my father had been killed in an ambush in Tunisia. His things were sent home, plus medals. I went to work that day but had to be taken home as I couldn't stop crying.

Judging from these experiences, it would be easy to assume that family life had been perfect before the war. Certainly those who had been married a short time felt they were leaving an idyllic world. But others, for whatever reason, were tired of family life and found a legitimate excuse to leave: 'I'm off to fight for my country.'

Rose Falkner's father escaped from an unhappy relationship and returned to even more problems than he had left:

I look back now at the age of fifty and know how different our family's life would have been if he hadn't returned at all.

My father was already in the ARP but signed up for active service when he found out my mother was expecting their third child – me. This ended an already rocky relationship between them. So, while he was off fighting for King and Country, Mum was left to keep the home fires burning. She had two children, was pregnant and was working in an ammunition factory.

After I was born, she met and fell in love with a young man. I understand the trend was to live for the day during the war years. Then she realised she was pregnant again, around the same time as a bomb landed on our house. We were all packed off to Lancashire, pushed from pillar to post. As soon as they realised Mum was expecting, we were shown the door. In all this she insisted we wouldn't be split up. We finally settled with a very nice family, who became life-long friends. They helped Mum through a difficult birth and looked after the five of us like we were their own. As young as I was, I can recall some very happy moments at that time.

Then VE Day – my father found out that we were in Lancashire and came to visit. Because Mum wanted nothing more to do with him, he up and left, taking my eldest brother and sister with him. It wasn't long after that Mum, my new brother and I were on our way home. We lived with my mother's sister and the eldest two lived with my father's sister. Although we were not together, at least Mum was able to see them. My father promised he would accept baby Michael as his own, to win Mum back. All Mum wanted was to be with her children.

We were rehoused by the council and given a flat in Dagenham. This proved to be the start of hell. Not only were there the hardships of little money and home comforts, you soon appreciated others' leftovers. Our good stuff was sold or pawned in order to obtain money for more needed items. On top of this there were the constant rows and fights between Mum and Dad.

My father started to take it out on baby Michael and Mum was expecting yet again. The rows got worse and Dad became more violent with Michael. He would find any excuse to smack him, but the smacks left marks. Mum realised what was going on and arranged for Michael to be placed in the care of Dr Barnardo's home in Ilford. Being local, she could visit him regularly and she knew he was safe. She was hoping things would improve and she could have him home again after she had my youngest sister. But things just got worse. As soon as Mum was getting on her feet again she fell pregnant for the sixth and last time and realised she wouldn't be able to bring Michael home. Her visits became more heartbreaking for her and it upset him to see his mum walk away from him. Dr Barnardo's, in all their wisdom, moved him to Kent. Mum couldn't afford the travel expenses plus looking after us. Father wasn't going to make any effort to help.

Her visits to Michael came to a halt. She had to make do with written words on his progress and the photos they sent. Time went by and my youngest brother was born. Things didn't improve between my mother and father. Then Mum found a way around it. We started to go hop picking for three weeks in the year. It was a working holiday for us kids and Mum made the most of the time in Kent, visiting Michael. As my father stayed at home to go to work, he didn't know about it. It was on one of these visits that Dr Barnardo's approached Mum about having Michael adopted. After a lot of soul searching, she made the heartbreaking decision to give him up. He was then six years old. From that day, she didn't see him again.

All through her life she never stopped talking about him. She hoped when he was older he would get in touch. We lost Mum ten years ago with cancer. We tried to contact Michael so Mum would get her wish, but with no luck.

Three years ago we were contacted by Dr Barnardo's and told

our brother was living in New Zealand, married with four children, and wanted to get in touch with his family. After a lot of letter writing, he and his wife flew into Heathrow. The reunion was wonderful. I'll never forget that day. It must have been the best day of our lives. He was the image of our mum. She would have been so proud of him. The only sad part was that he arrived six years too late to mend her broken heart. It's great to have him back in the family where he belongs.

My father is still alive, living with his brother. After a string of illnesses it has to be said that only the good die young.

Some fathers decided that they did not wish to return to the way of life they had left behind. It was bewildering for a child to be told that Daddy was not coming back. Was it because of something they had done?

Irene Beardshall was a baby at the start of the war:

I was a child with a father away at war. I was born in July 1939; my father went to war in September.

He was stationed in the Lake District – Cumbria. At first he came home on leave, then he started writing letters to my mother saying he could not get leave. When the time came at the end of the war he never came back, as he had met another woman where he was billeted.

I was twelve years old when he next came home. That was to see his father, my granddad, who was dying. The next time was when I was fourteen years old, for his brother-in-law's funeral. The next time I saw him was when I was twenty-three years old and he came to see his first grandchild, my daughter. I then saw him four times before he died four years ago. I have waited all my life for my father to come home to stay, but he never did.

The father of Daphne Irving (now Martin) was another who didn't come home for long:

My father, John Irving, was a Lieutenant RNVR, and my mother, Jessie, worked for the ARP at a casualty post. In 1942 or '43 my father was posted to South Africa.

He returned to England early in 1945 and we had no prior

warning of his coming. All I can remember is a knock on the door one evening and, when I went to open it, there was my father. I closed the door and went speechless to my mother.

'Well, who is it?' she asked.

I whispered, 'It's Dad!' – and I'd left him standing on the door-step!

Within a very short time of his homecoming my mother dis-covered that he had met another woman in South Africa and that he intended returning to her. My mother was devastated. She confided to me, years later, that she had wanted to put her head in the gas oven, but there were us children to be considered.

There are only three occasions I remember clearly from that time. One day when Dad took my brother, sister and me to Hampstead Heath Fair on Easter Monday, and another time, because he had forgotten my birthday – my thirteenth – my mother insisted he took me out for the day. On both these outings he was morose and preoccupied. He hardly spoke to us and we felt awkward and ill-at-ease in his company. The third memory is of his final goodbye in May 1945. My sister and I were sitting in church waiting for the service to begin when we were told to go outside to see our father. Outside the church were our parents; Mum told us to say goodbye to Dad because he was going back to South Africa. I don't recall what my father said. I know I said nothing. I refused to say goodbye.

In one respect it was a relief when he left, for we could get on with our lives, but things were very difficult for my mother. What little she received from my father in support payments, she had to fight for through solicitors and law courts, which she found very de-meaning and in the end she gave up. She became very bitter about my father, and this coloured her opinion of men in general. She had to work hard to support the family. If there was any government assistance in those days she was too proud to claim it. She died last October at the age of ninety and I believe the hurt was still with her. She never forgave my father.

As I see it now, we were just another casualty of the war. I often wonder where he is and whether he is still alive. I'd have liked to see him again.

Not all children had such unhappy experiences. Wendy Webb (now

Davey) lived in South London during the war. Her father was in the RAF:

He was posted out to India and I remember his censored letters arriving spasmodically. It was some time after VJ Day that he was demobbed and came back to us. I think the war years brought us closer together than ever. He had missed seeing my brother and me growing up and I think we felt we had to make up for those lost years somehow. He gave me my first 'grown-up' watch when he came home, long since beyond repair but still treasured. My father became my most trusted friend and ally, and remained so until his death in 1969.

Colin Moffatt was a teenager, living in Toronto, when the war was over. His father Jack was fighting overseas. They made a huge banner that read 'Welcome Home, Jack' and hung it across the verandah:

Suddenly Dad came home and we welcomed home this stranger. I must have been a surprise, too. When he left I was about four feet, ten inches tall and was six feet, two inches tall when he returned. There was a lot of water under the bridge during this time span, but we all were grateful that he came back in good health and mind. It was like removing a hundred-pound weight off our backs.

Sheila Ducat's parents and older sister had emigrated to Canada from Scotland in 1929. Her father had served in World War I and was forty-nine at the outbreak of number two. Although he was over age, the army responded to his pleas to be let in again. He joined the Royal Canadian Engineers, where the men called him 'Pop':

I remember the day Daddy came home to Winnipeg. At first, all I saw was khaki. I was five years old and vaguely remembered Dad's face, reinforced by snapshots from England, of course, but faint in my mind. Then this tall man picked me up for a hug. There was that darn khaki colour again. This man had white hair. Who was he? Did I know him? He evidently knew me. Then I looked closely at his eyes. They were a bright blue. Wow! My DAD! My back had been like a ramrod and then I was hugging him hard.

After that, the soldiers and their families were treated to tea and cakes in the main station. Every time Dad tried to move, there I was hanging on his leg like a limpet. I wasn't going to give him up again.

His boots intrigued me. The soles and heels were so thick. Alison, my sister, and Mom were laughing and talking and joking. I didn't understand any of the conversation. I just hugged his knees. It was wonderful!

When Margaret Povey's father went away, she was a little over a year old and obviously unable to remember him. She lived with her mother in a street of small, old-fashioned cottages where everyone knew each other and most of their business. Her mother's entire family lived in the same road – parents, two sisters and their respective families:

We were a tight little family circle which must have been a great help and comfort to my mother in the following traumatic years.

First my father's infrequent letters stopped altogether. Then the dreaded telegram saying that he was missing and finally the news that he had been traced as a Japanese POW on the Burma Railway. Then my mother received a few postcards that were printed by the Japanese with about four or five sentences each with a positive or negative response, i.e. I am well or I am not well. My father always ticked the favourable choice, in order to prevent worry at home, so although they were not a true indication of his health, they did confirm that he was still alive, whilst my mother was coping with the everyday difficulties of the war at home and raising a small child alone.

In the meantime, my father and his fellow prisoners were not informed that the war was over, their Japanese guards simply left one day with no explanation. The men searched for whatever food they could find, then simply took advantage of the unexpected rest. After some time, spotter planes began flying over the area, trying to pinpoint the men who were in isolated pockets in the jungle. They dropped first-aid equipment and various supplies with the message that the war was over and that they would return.

Return they did, using the airstrip the prisoners had been making for the Japanese.

My father said that their rescuers were a little nervous of

approaching them at first because they resembled half-starved savages. They were then taken to field hospitals for treatment before being put on a ship for home.

The ship sailed slowly home while the men were given nourishing food and the chance to rest and recuperate. One officer had the unhappy task of talking to the men to prepare them for children who would not know them and wives who would not necessarily be overjoyed to see them.

After disembarking from the ship, the men crowded on to the train for London, laughing, joking and full of high spirits. Yet the further they went the quieter they became and by the time they were approaching London they were absolutely silent, each man deep in his own thoughts, probably recalling the officer's words and wondering what sort of reception they were going to receive.

I was kept indoors when my father finally arrived home so that my mother could have those first precious moments to herself. And then suddenly he was there, strange and yet somehow familiar (I suppose the photograph had done the job). My first impression was of a soldier's uniform and a face more deeply tanned than I had ever seen before. But when he held out his arms to me it seemed perfectly natural to run to him to be picked up. His first words to me were 'Have you got a kiss for your dad?'

There seemed to be a lot of people in our house all talking at once. A young lad from across the road struggled in with my father's kit-bag, determined to prove everyone wrong in saying he would not be able to lift it (it weighed a ton). Later we had the excitement of unpacking it. I can remember a little leather handbag with pictures in it for me, and packets of sugar!

I followed him round like a shadow for days as he visited various friends and relatives.

My grandfather would come over to our house and sit at the kitchen table, chin cupped in his hands and say, 'Tell us about the war, Nobby.' And my father would keep us enthralled with stories of strange and wonderful things that he had seen or amusing incidents that had happened, but never about the horrors that he must have seen. But the malarial sweats and the bad dreams told a story of their own.

Sadly both my parents died many years ago, but I still have a few souvenirs to remind me of this wartime period: my father's medals, some newspaper cuttings, a tatty old wallet containing a photograph of my mother and myself that he carried all through the war, even burying it at times to prevent the Japanese from taking it. But probably the most precious, a letter from the wife of a fellow prisoner, thanking my father for helping her husband with his work, for, she says, without his help she would not have had a husband to return to her.

Barbara Birkenhead (now Saunders) was one of the very lucky ones. When her father came home, it created a wonderful memory which has comforted her ever since:

My brother was only twelve or thirteen when my dad went to war and when he returned he had a grown-up son, who by this time was serving an apprenticeship as a joiner. When I think back, life did seem hard for the two of them. The period of adjustment was disagreeable. My dad must have found it very hard to come to terms with the situation and my brother, who I suppose felt he was the man of the house, suddenly had to revert to being second in command.

From my own point of view, life was now complete. I had my dad back from the war and I was the first to see him again. Because the war was still on, existing servicemen coming back to England could not let their families know where they were. They just arrived on the doorstep.

It was Monday lunchtime and I had left school to go home for lunch. My friend came running after me and told me that my dad had just got off her bus. I turned and went back with her and there, coming around a bend, was my dad, complete with kit-bags, etc. I just simply threw myself at him and we both jumped around the pavement hugging and loving each other. Again, on reflection, he must have wondered who this gangling girl was rushing towards him as I, too, had grown up over four years. We arrived home and, of course, I ran into the house to tell my mum he was home. As she turned to answer me there he was in the living-room doorway and bump, down my mum went into a dead faint. When Dad went to see to Mum, the dog wouldn't let him near her and growled and grunted at him. It was utter chaos, but what a fantastic atmosphere.

On the night VE Day was announced, my mother had some fireworks in store and he went out on to the corner and, before the neighbours knew what had happened, there were rockets and fireworks going off and I remember it was quite a knees-up that night.

Unfortunately, my dad died in 1960 at the age of fifty-three and I lost one of the best friends a girl could have. We shared the same humour and laughed a lot together. Until the day I die I will feel the warmth and excitement of my dad's arms around me on that cold February lunchtime. Whenever I feel down I think of it and I get a great deal of comfort from the memory of that day.

6

A Home Away from Home

*A*S THE ALLIES *advanced through Europe, a large number of British women began to prepare themselves for a long journey. Like modern-day explorers, the war brides of World War II set their sights on a new life overseas. For them, 'coming home' meant travelling to a home they had never seen.*

With so many British servicemen posted overseas, the civilian female population had been starved of relationships with the opposite sex. The uniforms of men from other countries began to look more and more attractive. With a generosity that suggested limitless funds, the friendly invader from overseas was irresistible to a lot of young women.

As a result, thousands of girls followed the boys from camp to camp in the hopes of pursuing a relationship. Concerned at the number of 'camp followers' attending the dances at one American Air Force base in Hertfordshire, the American Red Cross decided to protect their homesick servicemen by making arrangements with the local Women's Voluntary Service. All the girls admitted to the dance were hand-picked, and the WVS chose only those they knew personally and considered to be of good standing.

Stories of Canadian and American servicemen being dragged into doorways by sex-starved British girls became part of popular myth-ology, no doubt perpetrated by angry fathers waiting for their daugh-ters to come home. Yet many of these encounters blossomed into romances.

With the constant threat of an overseas posting hanging over them, thousands of couples decided that the partner they had discovered at the dance or service canteen was the one with whom they wished to share their life. More than 40,000 Canadian servicemen and almost a million Americans stationed in Europe decided that they could not live without the girl they had met during their stay.

To a great many women who fell under the spell of these North American visitors, the future looked bright indeed, an opportunity to escape from the dismal, shabby, bomb-blasted island of their birth to a Hollywood land of plenty. Egged on by visions of sprawling Texan ranches, they eagerly accepted the proposals, only to discover that the luxury they had been led to expect was far from an accurate description of the home they eventually found.

Dorie Lloyd's husband had told her the truth about the area he came from in Canada. It was still a shock:

My infant daughter and I arrived in Halifax, Nova Scotia, on 24 November 1944, after a dreadful ten-day journey. Halifax was indeed a welcome sight. The Salvation Army took charge of us, taking us to a private home for the night and putting us on the right train the next morning. The train journey itself was an ordeal, wondering just where I was heading and what would be waiting for me at the end. My husband was still fighting in Italy and, although I had corresponded with my in-laws, I was still very nervous about meeting them.

As the train travelled northward and I looked out of the window, all I saw were trees and more trees. I wondered where on earth all the towns were. Here and there I saw a wooden house and prayed I wouldn't be living in something similar.

Arriving late at night at my destination in north-west New Brunswick, I stepped off the train and all I saw was a sea of faces. All the village, I believed, turned out to meet the train. My in-laws were there (all of them), but I was really too exhausted to take everything in.

The next day I knew I had stepped back fifty years in time: no indoor plumbing, going up a hill to pump a pail of water, a big monster sitting in the kitchen called a wood stove, no paved roads, in the spring up to your ankles in mud. The worst thing I found was the outdoor toilet, marching through the snow and sitting while the icy wind whistled around you know what. I learned to cope and by the time my husband arrived back in Canada I had settled in, more or less.

We began our married life together in a small wooden house and the early years were far from easy. The returning veterans were finding it hard to settle and a number of war brides just could not cope and returned to their own countries.

Doris Plourde worked in an operations room that had been bombed and was forced to move her quarters to the YWCA in Chichester, Sussex. It was nothing to the move she was about to make:

The Canadians were stationed all around the area. Periodically they would issue invitations for dances in their camp. I had one stripe up at that time and when they sent this big lorry to take the girls in I was put in charge. So off we went to Goodwood and it was in the winter and we had our big greatcoats on and I was the only one with a stripe. My future husband was in the cloakroom taking the coats. He took my overcoat and since he wasn't a dancer I never saw him as I was rounding up my troops and getting them back on the lorry.

Not too long after that I was at home in my village on seven days' leave and I was cleaning up my overcoat buttons and I put my hand in my overcoat pocket and here I pulled out a piece of paper and on the piece of paper was the name and address of the Canadian soldier who had taken my coat in the cloakroom. He then became my husband and that was the start of how I became a war bride and made a new home in Canada.

Not all British girls toured the camps looking for the man of their dreams. Many were already part of a camp. Peggy Chalklin joined the army in 1940:

There was a choice in those days when you were in England that you either joined the armed forces, the land army or the ammunitions factory. That was the choice that you had. I was living in Camberwell and was seventeen.

I met my husband in Llandrindod Wells, Wales. He was taking an officer-cadet training course and I was a driver there. I met him at a dance. As a matter of fact, he wasn't the one I had my eye on. No, but he came over and asked me to cut the rug and I didn't know what he was talking about. I looked at him and I said, 'I beg your pardon?' He said, 'How about cutting the rug?' and I wondered what he was saying. He said, 'Oh, that means having a dance,' and I said, 'Oh, yes, of course.' So we started to dance around the dance floor. He was in the Canadian Army and he was a little bit under the weather for drink because they were all out having a good time. He asked me if I would walk home with him and I said, 'Sure, I'll walk home with you and that's it, that's as far as it goes.' I was a little bit leery, you know, but I said I would walk him home anyway and he was a real gentleman, I must say. He fell down a couple of times and I had to prod him with his cane and I said, 'Come on, get up. You'll be getting into trouble if the army comes along and catches you.' Well, he finally got up and came to his senses and said, 'Oh, my God, I've had too much to drink.'

I said, 'Yeah, you can say that again,' because I'm a non-drinker.

Of course, I thought I'd never see him again, but the next week I was going on leave, and I didn't tell him I was going on leave, and then when I came back he had written to me at home and said he would meet me at a station. I was supposed to get off there to meet him but when I saw him there I thought, well, I'll fix you, I'll go on to the next station, which I did. I wanted to meet him but I wanted to make sure that he was going to be there. So, playing a game, I thought I'd go on to the next station, which I did. When I got back I met him in the NAAFI and he came over and he said, 'Where were you? I was at the station to meet you.' I said, 'I didn't see you.'

We sat there and we had a cup of tea and we sat there chatting. He wanted to see me the next night and that was it. It carried on and carried on and then he asked if he could marry me. That was in 1943 and we were married in 1944.

He told me about Canada off and on because my father was a Canadian. My mother loved him from the first time she saw him. She thought he was just wonderful. He told me about Canada and I was a little leery. He left England in November 1945 and I came out here in August 1946.

I had a little thirteen-month-old daughter when I came to Canada. We had to go to Folkestone to get the boat. I never saw so many ATS people and armed women in all my life and kids screaming and bawling. I was discharged then. There were loads of other war brides there. It was a war-brides ship, the *Queen Mary*. That ship was really packed.

I was very sick on the trip over because they gave us white bread and we hadn't been used to having white bread; we'd been eating black bread for years. We never knew what it was like having all these syrupy desserts and whipped cream; it was so rich for our systems. Most of us up-chucked over the side. It was good going down; it wasn't so good coming back!

At that time, most of the seamen had a lot of nylons and, of course, we hadn't seen nylon stockings for the whole time the war was on. They would get them from the forces that were going over and we were buying them like crazy.

It wasn't too bad with a small child because there was a nursery on board and the Red Cross people were absolutely fabulous. I can't say enough for them; they were absolutely wonderful.

First of all, we had to dock at Halifax. We were in Halifax for two days because of the fog. The boat couldn't dock to get us off and on the train in Halifax.

When we finally docked the train wasn't ready, so they told us that we could walk around Halifax, which, of course, we did with our babies.

When we got to Toronto it was a madhouse at Union Station. We'd been on the train for two days. We threw an awful lot of paper diapers out the window along the way. That was our main fun because we had no way of washing diapers. They handed us these paper diapers and we didn't know what they were; we'd never seen anything like that before. Of course, when we started to use them we thought they were absolutely super. When they were soiled we were throwing them out the window of the train. What could you do with them? There were no facilities on the train.

My husband was there at Union Station in Toronto to meet me.

He was in civilians. Believe me, I didn't recognise him. He had on a grey pinstripe suit and a fedora. They called my name out and they called his name out and I guess he'd been looking at me for a while and I stood looking at him for a while and I thought, God, that's not him. That can't be him. But anyway it was him. 'I'm sorry,' I said. We'd been writing to each other for fourteen months, but I hadn't seen him.

I was very nervous when I first met his parents. They didn't treat me very kindly and the only one that did was his older brother. I felt very strange and my accent was a little bit more broad then. They resented the fact that I had stolen their son because he had had a girlfriend over here and his mother really wanted him to marry her. I think it was because her father had a business.

The war brides were treated very badly when we came to Canada. We were spat on, we were jeered at by the people in Toronto. As soon as you spoke they would say to you, 'Are you one of those?' I'd look at them and I'd say, 'I beg your pardon?' 'Are you one of those English war brides?' and I'd say, 'Yes, as a matter of fact I am.' 'Well, why don't you go back to your own bloody country and leave our boys alone? You stole our boys.' That was what was said all the time. And I think that was the reason that most of the girls went back, because they didn't get the proper treatment that they thought they were going to get and their husbands didn't stick by them. Mine did, fortunately.

We had two children and we've been married for forty-six years. We've got three grandchildren.

Rene Lund was one of many war brides who heard that the war was over on board the MV Athlone Castle bound for Canada:

We didn't know whether to laugh or cry. Here we were in the middle of the Atlantic, when we would have loved to have been in the middle of Trafalgar Square! On board the ship were war brides, young airmen on their way to take part in the Empire Training Scheme and even some German prisoners.

The captain issued a bottle of beer for us to celebrate VE Day and those of us who were non-drinkers lowered our beer bottles over the side and down to the air force boys below. I think we used our precious nylons, well aware that there were more to be had in our new homeland on the horizon.

My husband and I were reunited in Winnipeg at the end of September 1945 and had a very, very happy life together with our two wonderful adopted children until he died in 1977. I still miss him so much.

Florence Irving was in the armed services and decided to visit a club with a friend. Her husband-to-be had the same idea:

He was a very shy man, didn't drink or anything like that . . . And this other soldier he had met on the train said, 'Let's go into one of the clubs.' They came into the New Zealand Club in London and I was on a twenty-four-hour pass. I'd been home to see my parents and had met some of the girls and we had gone up to the club to sit and have a drink. He came in and the fellow he was with held up what I thought was a bottle of lager or something and I'm saying to my friend, 'Don't mix with them; they're Canadians; they're hot blooded.' That's what my parents had told me. See, I was on a mixed gun site with what they called the wheelchair cases. You know, they were all pretty old to us young girls. Anyway this Canadian came up and said, 'May I sit down?' so I said, 'Well, this is still a free country', very aloof like, and that's how we met. We seemed to hit it off right away.

We got married in 1945 before he left to go back to Canada. I waited to join him and told the authorities that I wanted to be there with him for my first wedding anniversary. They got me on a ship called the *Aquitania*. There must have been over 2000 war brides on the ship, about thirty-two to a cabin. But we were treated wonderfully. There were soldiers down on the lower deck, but that was all wired off. We weren't supposed to associate with them, but I'm afraid some of the girls did. If they were caught, their husbands were notified and if the husbands said, 'No, I don't want a girl that's running around or been untrue', or anything like that then when we got to Canada they were put on another ship and sent back. Several of them were.

We got off the boat at Halifax and transferred to trains. I was heading for a place called Allen Water in northern Ontario, which was between Armstrong and Sioux Lookout. I had three days and nights on the train. On the way they would drop off the various war brides, some with new babies, at different points along the route. Lots of them were sent on a lot further than me, to Winnipeg and Vancouver. Some ended up on Indian reservations and God knows where.

Anyway, the train pulled into Allen Water and I got out. There was just the railway track and a small store. My husband's mother, sisters and a lot of Indians who had been out trapping were standing there. They had heard that John's new wife was paddling herself across the ocean and would be arriving on the train. Of course, John was there and his mother and his father, half cut as usual.

My husband had been very honest and not only told me what to expect but had told my mum and dad. It was just all bush, no roads, no streets, just the railway track going off into the distance and a general store that a Mr Gasby ran for the Indians and about ten white families that were scattered through the area. Anyway, we all headed for home. John had got a little Hudson Bay cottage for us. It was old and had three bedrooms, but John had done it up and had furnished it. My parents had said, 'We don't care but, whatever happens, we want to see pictures of how our daughter is living, the furniture and home.' So he had had the furniture shipped in.

Unfortunately John's family's attitude to me was terrible. His two sisters got me on the quiet after a few days and said, 'Within six weeks we'll have you on that boat back to England. We don't want you around. Why should our brother marry someone from another country?' They said the British were no good and stuff like that and that they had heard about girls who had been in the military, being the officers' groundsheet. Oh, they had it all off pat. I would just look at them, do a silly grin and stand up for my rights. And when our first baby was born they had no love at all for the baby.

The food would come in twice a week to the general store and they used to break the ice on the lake and put it in an ice house through the winter. I'd come from London into this and, I know it sounds strange, but I was young and adventuresome and figured that you made your life wherever you decide to. I was a little homesick on and off but, as my mother had always said, 'When you marry you make your life with whomever you choose.' And remember, we were in love and continued to be right up to the time he died in 1989.

John Craig had been an anti-tank sergeant in an infantry battalion, the Argyll and Sutherland Highlanders of Canada, for five years. When the war finally ended in Europe he breathed a sigh of relief. At last he could get back to the girl he had met while stationed in Scotland:

After living like an animal in holes dug in the ground for so long, the sudden freedom was exhilarating.

At the end of the war I was twenty-three years old. During my training period in England I had visitied Scotland, the land where my mother and father had been born. One day a buddy of mine told me there were seven women to every man in Dundee. With odds like that I figured it would be a great place for a young soldier to spend a few days. On one of my visits I met a young Scottish girl with rosy cheeks and beautiful red hair. We became engaged but fate stopped us from getting married, as her father died on my last leave.

I came home on the *Queen Elizabeth* with thousands of other returning Canadian veterans and immediately began job-hunting in the Niagara area.

I had to pay for my future wife's passage to this country, but it was the best investment I ever made. She also sailed the Atlantic aboard the *Queen Elizabeth* and we were married in 1947. A boy and two girls soon followed and now, in our twilight years, we have six grandchildren to bring us joy.

War is a terrible waste and an experience I have never forgotten, but it also had some happy endings. If Hitler had not invaded Poland I would have never visited Dundee, Scotland, to beat the odds of seven to one.

Marjorie Mounter almost became a war bride. When she was seventeen she met and fell in love with a member of the Royal Canadian Air Force. His name was Rex and he soon asked her to marry him:

In May 1945 I got a letter from Rex to say he was in Bournemouth prior to going home to Canada on leave. He was going to come to Plymouth for the weekend and then cancelled it. His family were against him marrying me. His mother refused to write to me and told him to wait until he'd been home for six months and, if he still felt the same, he could send for me. He said he would talk them around to his way of thinking. The plan was that we hoped to marry in the autumn and I would get a transfer to the CWRNs and get shipped back to Canada.

Well, that was the last I heard from him. To the end of my life I shall always wonder why. To be left with no word at all was cruel, much more upsetting than a 'Dear John'.

I met an old acquaintance when I went home on leave in September. He was in the Royal Navy, stationed at Plymouth, and we started dating. I wasn't over enthusiastic as I still lived in hope of hearing from Rex. Even after we married, for years there was a large part of my heart missing. To this day I would love to know what happened.

Audrey Rosebush had known her Canadian husband for ten days before they were married:

It all seemed so perfect and even more perfect with the birth of our daughter, Patricia, the following July. My husband served with the Royal Canadian Engineers, First Division.

When Pat was about eight months old there was some military talk that my husband Alvin was to return to Canada for some special training, so he applied for permission for us to go with him. After much paperwork, medicals and checking my character for security . . . I then received an exit permit. We were warned not to inform anyone of our leaving, so I stayed with my parents, suitcases packed and waiting for the telegram that gave you twelve hours to be in Liverpool. I'm leaving my home, family, friends and crossing the Atlantic where the U-boats were still active, with a small child and going to a strange country and strange people.

Our ship was unescorted. She was the *Louis Pasteur*, at that time the fourth fastest ship in the world. We had approximately twenty war brides, three children, 1503 German Africa Corps prisoners –

the balance were Canadian Armed Forces, wounded or going home for special training. The army, in its strange way, decided my husband could do his special training somewhere in Scotland, so I went alone to Canada with Pat.

I was met in Toronto by my father-in-law and two sisters-in-law. It was cordial, but I was an intruder. I had married their brother/son and as with most war brides it was assumed we had stolen their men.

Now, after almost two years, Al was coming home. Would he be the man I had married but really not spent a lot of time with? Would he want me? Would he want to get to know his daughter? I was not sure I would recognise him when the train pulled into the Pure Foods Building in the Exhibition Grounds in Toronto. My fears were groundless. He saw me first and from that first hug and kiss I knew we would be able to see our dreams slowly come true. All the loneliness was worthwhile, all the squabbles with in-laws, finding a place of my own and paying half of my army allowance for two rooms, as well as discrimination because I was English.

During the waiting years there were some awful times and some so funny only a Limey could see the funny side. Like the time I shared a flat with a girl who came over on the same ship. We were in a small town and somehow people assumed we were both married to the same man . . . Can you imagine two city girls moving on to a farm and looking after the picking of ten acres of strawberries and ten acres of sweet-corn? Neither of us had ever used a cookstove or seen an outhouse, yet we managed. We hired pickers, paid them and made sure the produce was shipped where instructed.

I think the worst part of waiting was the boredom. In Toronto at that time there was little, if any, theatre, only movies. I did attend some song recitals at the Eaton's College Street store. I did miss the easy availability of theatre or music hall as we knew it.

The thing I want people to realise is that it was not only tough for the men coming home. It was tough for families where the men had been gone for five years. Everyone had grown older. They had set their own routines and now this stranger had come home and a new routine had to start, not only for his family but for him. The military had made all his decisions for him and now he had to try to make the right decisions for his family and without rocking the boat. So it was difficult for everyone. If there was a real foundation of love, trust and faith you made it. I was one of the lucky ones.

7

Goodbye, Rosie – Hello, Doris

*I*T HAD BEEN *a war like no other. Civilians in Britain had been called on to withstand the enemy onslaught as never before. But in one important respect, World War II did resemble World War I – in the need for total mobilisation, both of the military and of the nation's industrial strength. World War I had given women the opportunity to leave their homes and play their part in securing a victory. In 1939, this opportunity presented itself again. Women could enter military auxiliary services or train for technical and scientific jobs. Encouraged by the government, women eagerly filled the spaces vacated by men who had been called away to war.*

Working conditions became more favourable to women as new mechanical processes of production developed. This had a direct bearing on the status of women in industry, but brought with it two fundamental problems.

The first was that many of the jobs now competently handled by women had, of course, belonged to men in the armed services. These men had been promised that their jobs would be waiting when they returned, which put female employees out of work again. The second problem was the issue of equal pay for equal work, by no means the norm in the 1940s. Although wartime industries had made some progress in applying this principle, it was not automatically carried over when hostilities ended.

Once the service personnel were demobilised and millions of male workers returned to the job market, women suddenly found them selves discarded. The traditional 'women's jobs' – nursing, social service and domestic work – were extremely lowly paid, since few organised trade unions had penetrated these fields. But women had done what their country asked them to do – left their homes or jobs less crucial to the war effort to work in the factories. They had been trained and the money was good; they had been able to buy whatever they wanted (if it was available) without having to scrounge around for 'that little bit extra'.

In September 1941, a desperate government had threatened to send unemployed women without dependents to prison if they refused war work. Once the war was over they applied tremendous pressure to force them back into the home. To quote from the documentary film The Life and Times of Rosie the Riveter, *wartime magazine recipes had been short and simple to prepare; in 1945 'suddenly recipes took whole days'. Women who had been constantly bombarded with the message that it was impossible to win the war without them were now told that 'real' women stayed at home and made babies. Their position was made even more difficult with the closure of many of the crèches, day nurseries and nursery schools that had been set up during the war.*

But the upheaval in women's lives brought about by the war had left them with a broader group of friends, looser ties with their communities and greater independence. Although the ATS was given a mandate to 'turn the barrack-trained minds to a softer, domestic scene' and provided courses in arranging flowers, making cushions and curtains, and cooking for four instead of for hundreds, this was not what many women wanted. They had tasted the freedom of the outside world and were anxious to stay there and taste some more.

Of course, this feeling was not universal. Those with a factory job they had found boring were often quite happy to pass the role of breadwinner back to their returning husbands. But for those whose lives had taken on new meaning once they were given a challenging job, the suggestion that they step aside understandably caused resentment. Women who had been at home or working in a job that isolated them from others found companionship they had never known before as they worked alongside new-found friends. A 1943 survey found that as many as three-quarters of professional women wanted to keep their jobs after the war.

Muriel Hargreaves left a pre-war civil service clerical job to become an electrician during the war, filling a man's space at the Royal Ordnance factory at Chorley:

Sheer physical effort plus wartime rations did wonders for my figure, but my fair hands assumed the look of leather. I enjoyed all of it. The big thing it did for me and many more women was to open a whole new world to us. We realised there were so many things we could do, long before the words women's lib were uttered.

I have seen very clearly that the Second World War made a far bigger impact on women than the First. Before I was born, my mother worked on the railway during World War I and then went back to the same old grind. Not for my generation. We looked for more and went for it.

Mavis Young (now Drake) was in the land army and had grown to love the countryside:

Plans were already afoot to obtain my release from the land army. I returned to my work with a heavy heart, and although I knew I had no option, as I had to go home to nurse my sick mother, I was shattered when my release came through. I kissed all my friends goodbye, with the usual promises to write and visit, which I was able to do now and again. The adjustment to city life was long and painful, and when my mother finally recovered her health, I went into secretarial work, but I was only happy when I was able to escape to the countryside and wide open spaces at weekends and holiday times. And at our reunions it isn't the hard work, long hours and early rising we talk about most, but the humour of the many situations we found ourselves in, the friends we made, the patriotism, and most of all, of our pride in a job well done.

In other words, a new breed of woman discovered that her role in life had been that of a second-class citizen, and she was no longer prepared to devote herself exclusively to the wishes of her man. The government, however, stuck to the view that women should concern themselves with homes and children, while men went back to being the wage-earners, responsible for the financial welfare of their wives and families.

Rosie Longman was twenty years old, engaged to be married and living with her parents at the outbreak of the war. She worked in an aircraft factory until her fiancé returned from a POW camp in 1943 and they were married:

I took another job with less pay that allowed me to be at home and near him until his health improved. We had a son in 1945 and I stopped working outside the home and took in lodgers instead.

When the war was over I missed the companionship of the war and the knowledge that I was doing something worthwhile with my life. After the war I was 'Mummy', 'my daughter', 'my wife' or 'the landlady'. I was never me.

My husband also found it extremely difficult to adjust. Deaf from the dive-bombing and other noises on Crete, he missed his mates from the POW camp and, fed up with the female chatter of my land-girl lodgers, he would find some consolation with ex-servicemen at the British Legion on Saturday and Sunday nights.

I can imagine many marriages cracked under the strain. We were mostly married strangers after six years apart. It had left such a large hole in our lives at what should have been the best years.

I missed having my girlfriends to talk things over with and the friendly company we had always had at weekends during the war, and also felt resentful at not being able to afford to go to the cinema.

I bitterly regret the six lost years of the war, which took away the best years of our lives, except for the actual experiences of the friendliness of the time (that has now disappeared forever). I wouldn't have missed that for anything!

Sylvia Childs worked in an ambulance station during the five years her fiancé was in the Middle East:

We corresponded all that time. One Saturday evening in January 1945, quite out of the blue, I received a telegram saying he had landed in Liverpool. His name had been picked from a hat as the only one from his regiment to be granted one month of home leave. He still says it is the only raffle he has ever won.

We became engaged during that leave and were married after he was sent home again in May 1946. We lived with my in-laws for four years.

As for myself, the disbanding of the ambulance station was a very sad time. I was going to miss the camaraderie. I still think of it with nostalgia.

The future Mrs Peggy Boorman's husband was called up at the outbreak of war, having been in the Territorial Army:

They all joined up and enjoyed the war, going out most nights on the town wherever they were.

We were married in 1943. I carried on working and dodging the bombs on London. The boys came home on leave, all went out to the pubs, left the wives at home, of course.

When the war ended, luckily most of them returned OK, but it was still all boys together. Then the babies came along. Not much money, most lived with parents, no proper jobs. None of them had really grown up, didn't take their responsibilities properly. It was Mum, army, then the wives who took over.

Now they have mostly retired, not much pension, hopefully the wife will keep on working for a little longer, enough money to go down to the Legion for a drink or two with the Old Boys to talk over the Old Days.

One wonders what life would have been without the war.

Canadian Dorothy Lutz went to Halifax and was accepted in a war-emergency electric welding course:

When we finished the course we had to go to the Halifax shipyards to work. I was sixteen and the youngest welder in Canada at that time. I went to the pipe shop to work where you had to use bare rods, the hardest things to contend with. I really enjoyed it. I worked down in the holds of ships a few times, welding. It was very hard breathing because there were no ventilators like today. It was great working with the others.

We were told when we started at the Halifax shipyards that we had to give our jobs up to the men when they came back. They said, 'Now, look, girls, you are going to go down there to work, but when Joe and Tom and Bill come back from overseas you have to give them your job if they're qualified.' Unfortunately I got pneumonia from inhaling a lot of smoke from down in the holds and other places where there wasn't much ventilation. I spent all winter home sick. When I came back to work my job was already gone to a man.

I couldn't get another job welding – that was out. The men were all back and that was it. I didn't resent it then and still don't. I tried everywhere and I finally I got a job at a lunch counter.

Linda Wigley, another Canadian, also found that the end of the war did little to bring happiness:

The before and after war years were equally upsetting, as before the war we walked in the steps of the Great Depression and after the war we had to take a step backwards. The war, which was so unfair to many, gave others, especially women, the opportunity to escape the stereotype existence of going, for many at fifteen, to work at menial, low-paying jobs or marrying while very young. After experiencing four and a half years of the good life while working in a war plant – being royally treated, receiving top pay and benefits, it was devastating to suddenly have it all come to an end.

With all former war-plant workers and service personnel returning to the work force, it was almost impossible to find work, especially for one whose education did not extend further than grade eight level.

It took several months of desperate searching but I finally found employment at the Continental Can Company in Etobicoke, Ontario. After four and a half years of working short hours (albeit three shifts), it was a strain returning to the long ten-hour shift with lower wages and clocked timetables.

Joyce Hampson was drafted into the Morris engines factory during the war to work as a capstan operator, making gears for army trucks and tanks:

All of us women who worked there were quite aware that it was only for the duration, so felt no resentment when we were made redundant at the end of the war. We knew that we had just manned the machines whilst our menfolk were fighting.

I liked that work and the free and easy atmosphere of the factory, so, when I was sent back to my previous work, that I did resent. No way did I want to work under the conditions that I had pre-war. So it was with very bad grace that I went back and I can honestly say that it's the only time I have ever shirked on a job. The Essential

Works Order was lifted in 1946, so I lost no time in shaking the dust off my feet and left the place the same day that I'd heard on the 7 a.m. news that the order had been lifted.

Naturally, many women were happy to leave the factories to return to domestic life. They not only felt it was their duty to step aside for the returning servicemen, but were indeed anxious to settle down to the role of mother and housewife.

Carol Cockburn O'Neill, a Canadian girl, found that most of her friends felt the same way she did:

In September 1940, at age eighteen, I was offered my first job in the Toronto office of a firm building Hawker Hurricanes. In 1944 I was transferred to Fort William, Ontario, as purchasing expediter and lived in the residence built to house the many female welders and riveters brought in from across Canada.

However, when the war ended in 1945, the girls were happy to return to their homes to await the boys from overseas! I never met one girl in those five years who didn't want to get married, stay home and raise a family. Growing up in the '30s we were raised with that in mind. The word career wasn't in our vocabulary.

Oh, yes, I did meet one career woman while at Fort William – Elsie MacGill, North America's first woman aeronautical engineer. Now that was a career! Miss MacGill was an exception.

During the war Gemma Hodge had worked in the office of a food shop, doing food-office returns from ration-cards and also doing deliveries and working in the shop. She loved the work and enjoyed the company of her colleagues as well as all the interesting people she met:

When my husband came home we were like strangers. It took an awful long time for us to settle down to a completely different life and for me to give up my job and leave the girls I had worked with for so many years. It was a very difficult time, to say the least. Having had my own way of life for so long, I was reluctant to give it up to be a housewife.

Pat Beasley, whose husband had been away for four years, was glad to be able to leave her civilian job:

As soon as my husband came home I said, 'No more. I'm just not working any more.' I just gave up and he didn't want me to go to work either. But by 1949 I was working in the post office.

I wasn't naughty during the war, but I still liked to go dancing and we used to go to the cinema. Most nights we were out and I just couldn't accept that now I was going to be in. This is what was the trouble, you see. When he came home I thought, Well, no way can I stay and cook your meals because I'd been going out. Suddenly that stopped.

For Ivy Edgington, the end of the war finally brought her family together once more, but:

I would say that with my husband's return from the army, and my two children from evacuation, I was once again the humble housewife.

May Robertson decided to do something different:

My husband could not settle after he was demobbed and told me he was joining up again. So I packed my bags and went all over the world with him and my two children.

Hilda Marter felt the war was an important period in her life, and to this day thinks she missed an opportunity:

I served with the ATS in a heavy anti-aircraft regiment, for four years. My husband, whom I had married ten months before the war was declared, was called up only three months into the conflict. He was then sent to the Middle East where he spent the next four years.

I was sent to a munitions factory which I found very boring, doing the same sort of thing in the same sort of way, day in and day out. So when I saw a poster asking women to volunteer for war service, I signed on straight away. After training on three different sites, we were finally sent to a posting on the River Tees near Middlesbrough. Then followed other moves to various sites including Scotland, Biggin Hill and Northern Ireland. During my army life I saw quite a lot of action on gun sites, especially when we were stationed on the River Tees, and again, near Biggin Hill. I met many different people from many different backgrounds, which I would probably never have met had there not been a war. I had an important job, on the command post, that I enjoyed and the feeling of being my own person – instead of a housewife pandering to my husband's every need, which was the norm in those days – was a tremendous feeling and gave me a confidence I had never had before.

When my husband returned home from the Middle East I had already served four years in the ATS and had made many friends. Our unit was due to be posted to Belgium at any time, which I looked forward to eagerly. As soon as my husband came to see me at my site, on his disembarkation leave, he naturally expected me to ask for leave, which I did. I was granted a four-week leave, but forbidden to move too far out of the area because of the impending move to Belgium.

In those days, especially after a four-year absence, asking one's husband to use a condom was tantamount to asking for a divorce. It was considered to be the husband's decision. I, of course, never had a choice. My husband did not even consider my feelings on the subject. I was angry when I realised I was pregnant a few weeks later. I was very upset at having to leave all my friends and the life I loved, but I would never have considered an abortion, even if it had been legal, which it wasn't. I felt at the time that it was grossly unfair, that any plans a woman may have had for after the war, can be changed in a few moments, whether she wants them changed or not, just because she is a woman and expected to behave as her husband wishes.

I am, of course, only speaking of the times as they were then, thank goodness, it is vastly different now. I came out of the forces with nowhere to live, no knowledge of motherhood and before I had the baby, my husband was sent to Europe for a further nine months. My son was two months old before my husband saw him. I had to live in an ancient, broken down cottage, without proper electricity, no proper sanitation, no cooking facilities and miles away in the country. I even had to dig a hole for a toilet, which had a rickety screen erected around it.

My son grew into a healthy boy who is now, of course, a family man. I often wonder what sort of career I might have been able to follow had I been able to choose my own destiny.

Vicky Masterman served with the ATS during the war. She was from Glasgow, but was posted in England.

I found it quite difficult to adjust because I was a sergeant-major in charge of over a thousand girls. I missed the companionship plus authority. If I'd hadn't been in the army I'd never have the confidence that I have now. As for my husband, we had a very good relationship because he was a very quiet man, so I just took over automatically, running the house and bringing up the children. He was quite content in that way.

Lillian Wright Nisbet was in the Royal Canadian Air Force (Women's Division) during the war:

Most women donned uniforms as a form of back-up help for male family members or male friends in uniform in theatres of war. We had been doing whatever we could to help the war effort, such as participation in St John's Ambulance, the Red Cross and knitting.

Some of us had different ideas and I embarked on a lesson plan to learn how to fly. Shortly afterwards the RCAF began accepting women for ground crew and several of us joined.

When we returned home after the war, the impetus for such jobs as flying had left us. With the return of so many pilots we knew that we would have little chance of obtaining employment in a field so dominated by men. Money was scarce after years of air-force pay and some of us embarked on further education and others chose immediate marriage.

We were happy that the war was over, but it was unsettling to return to a world in which we were no longer considered as competitive in either the work force or general living. We had had to be better than the men to win promotion, but lost that chance once our uniforms went into the cedar chest. Since then we have waged an uphill fight for earned equality.

For Pamela Moncrieff joining the services was wonderful:

'Tis an ill wind, they say, and, for me, the war and joining the service was the highlight of my life and perhaps the happiest time of my life. I did not only join up to 'do my bit' but to escape a very mundane existence of being a companion to Mummy.

I came from what, I suppose, one would call an upper-middle-class family, private school and all that and, I suppose, looking back, I was a bit of a snob. I went into the services as a snob and came out a human being. It was marvellous meeting people from all walks of life and coming to know that you didn't have to be born with a silver spoon in your mouth to have hopes, dreams, feelings and fears, and that we are all, in fact, created equal. I never acquired a rank, other than a period I was given a stripe while serving as a driving instructor. I was having too much fun being humanised, having fun with 'ordinary' people.

For a period, also, I was an ambulance driver attached to Prittlewell Hospital, Southend. I had a mate, a very nice young man about my age, who obviously hadn't had the advantages in his life that I had had. We were real buddies and had many a laugh and giggle together, especially over our rather formidable sergeant-major.

When the war was over, home I went to resume my humdrum life again, but with a deal more self-confidence and assertiveness. During this period our TV broke down and we had to send for a repairman. Imagine who appeared, to my delight and surprise – my buddy from Southend. But things had changed. Although I was delighted to see him and all but welcomed him with open arms and started to chat away about our times together, he was very much on guard. He acted as the tradesman who must not be familiar with the daughter of the house. To me it was so sad that, although I felt completely comfortable and at ease with him, he did not with me. It struck me as a tragedy that we had gone through so much to break down so many barriers and they were gradually being put up again.

I never got brainwashed to go back to my 'station' and have always been grateful for the war for what I learned and have ever since remained a champion of the underdog.

Elaine Campbell was eighteen when she joined the Royal Canadian Air Force. By the time she was twenty she was in charge of radio personnel and gave bearings to pilots training on Mosquito bombers on the east coast of Canada:

We took a course in all of the technical aspects of radio on receivers and transmitters. We had to understand not only how they worked but be able to decipher the drawings. It was highly secret equipment at that time and quite technical. Added to this we had to be very quick because the pilots that were asking for a bearing were sometimes running out of fuel and not sure where they were. It was quite demanding because you could tell from their voices that they were pretty scared. They didn't have much gas and had to land somewhere. So it was essential that you were not only fast, but accurate.

All of our radio equipment was in a silo in a field at the end of the runway. I was in charge of that silo. In charge of all of the personnel that worked there. I was also working the equipment giving bearings to the pilots.

At the end of the war I went to university for three years to get my degree. I got my BA, then went to apply for my first job and what was the first question asked by the first person that interviewed me? 'Can you type?'

Jenny Booth was made aware at an early age which of the sexes was considered more important:

I was a child at grammar school at the end of the war, excitedly working towards matriculation and coming top in everything except French. I was hauled in front of the headmistress when I had done two years' work in algebra in two weeks. She told me off and said, 'It doesn't matter how clever you are, you will not get a place in a university for years. All the places are being saved for ex-servicemen. Even if they have no exams they are to get priority.' It was a hammer blow to me and I have never recovered. I feel it was a terrible waste.

She was right. I had to continue my studies on a day-release and evening-class basis. My parents thought it was only fair — they were not very keen on having a clever female in the family!

My parents had problems. My mother had taken over my pa's job when he went into the army and had to take a back seat on his return. His health never really got over some of the privation he had suffered. Her ego never got over the bruising it took having to step down in the business.

Pam Buckland was seventeen when she volunteered for the Women's Auxiliary Air Force in 1944. After two years' service she decided to leave:

I was confident that I would return to my former job as manageress of the library department in the local cash chemist, but I married before being demobbed in 1946, which meant that I no longer qualified as permanent staff, this being only applicable to single members.

It soon became obvious that I was never going to see eye-to-eye with my replacement and after several clashes of temperament I decided to go into private service. My parents were already employed in the capacity of cook and butler by Major and Mrs Neville Blond, so when offered the post of lady's maid to the mistress of the house, I didn't hesitate. Normally, of course, one works up to such an exalted position from the lower orders and after a long apprenticeship – but if Madam was prepared to take on an untried and inexperienced domestic, I was more than willing to do my best to please.

It wasn't always easy.

Life in the forces had offered little in the way of glamour or excitement, though to be fair, it had its moments. From serving King and Country, I was now serving the rich and famous, to my mind infinitely preferable.

My recently acquired husband had been posted to the Far East within a couple of months of marriage, which seemed a bit unfair – we'd barely had time to enjoy the conjugal delights afforded by short or weekend leaves. When he eventually returned to Civvy Street, Mrs Blond also co-opted him on to the staff. Back from Malaya on Friday and all kitted out as second butler within two days!

Doreen Michell had joined the Canadian Women's Auxiliary Corps and had returned home to a husband-to-be who had been a P O W. She found it easy to settle:

I was very lucky. My husband was very considerate. He always helped me with the dishes.

A. Freeman was in her twenties and like thousands of others, stood on a railway station and said goodbye with a new baby in her arms:

It was six years later that we saw him again. The 'little woman' had had to grow up fast, and the hard way. Living near bomber country over those years, it was a time of daily tensions. My baby was a few weeks old when I lost my home and so it had been a time of survival. In the beginning we were hungry and had no money, but I protected these children as best I could to be free and happy little kids.

I went to work part-time. My sister and I lived together and she cared for my little one with her three. I can look back now and truthfully say they were happy years, if we could only have had no loss of life.

Alas, not so with the returning of these strange men who came back as if nothing had changed. Once again, he was the master of the house and the children were expected to know and understand who this stranger was, other than the face in the photograph.

It was a traumatic time for the wife: the loss of one's own independence as the part-time job had to go, having to ask for any decision, being told what you can and cannot do.

Alas, they were the worst years of my life. It was not the men's fault. They had to lose those years. The women worked hard to save their marriages and to adjust the children to their fathers.

The loving, caring bonds that were created as a family in those wartime days between the mothers, grandmothers and the cousins have remained throughout the four generations. So, on reflection, it was all worthwhile.

Marie Lewis was unable to continue working after the war:

I had to go without so much. Looking back on it all today, I know it was well worthwhile. War was over, the coloured flags and lights we had had for our street parties were packed away and we looked forward to a brave, new, peaceful world!

I had worked on my local railway through the Blitz, replacing a chap who had gone into the RAF. Sadly enough, he didn't come home again, but I was unable to continue the job as a porteress because I had made my own contribution to the future and produced a son, the child I had wanted in my six years of marriage.

Mind you, I wouldn't have been able to have him enter the world so promptly for the victory celebrations if it hadn't been for the bomb that dropped at the end of our road in July 1944 when my soldier husband was home on leave. Our bedroom ceiling came down and showered us with debris. You can say the world really moved for us! My son was a direct result of enemy action . . . He was well and truly the only good thing that emerged from World War II for me.

The day after he was born, in April 1945, I sat up in bed and read the headlines of my newspaper: ALLIES ENTER BERLIN. While they were fighting that battle, I had been fighting my own private battle. They won and so did I!

A tiny poem helped Dorothy Lowman make a new beginning:

We who went through all the war years in danger zones, who experienced the dangers, the hardships, the sorrows, the tears mingled with sometimes laughter in unexpected places, felt restless and unsettled after the last all-clear.

As a midwife in hospital, delivering babies, wearing a tin hat instead of a uniform cap, the crucial part of the delivery often happened just as the terrible engines of the doodlebugs had cut off and there were fifteen seconds before the explosion, one knew not where. In a particular way it had become a way of life, so choosing another stage was not easy. I loved the East Enders, with their wit, their generosity and, above all, their courage.

Casually turning the pages of a book, I read: 'A rut is but a grave begun. Climb out, my friend, or else you're done.' Those words affected me and within a month I was in Austria, a civilian attached to the army. After three months in Graz, I was posted to Vienna, which was occupied by the four powers: the Russians, Americans,

French and the British. There were no bombs or air-raids, but restrictions and apprehension.

The apprehensions and the little fears seemed to cure my restlessness. I was there for the last three years of its occupation. I saw the treaty signed which made Austria a neutral country and saw the British flag lowered for the last time. I was sad to leave, but one could never forget our London war – a battle which changed so many lives.

8

Away with the Khaki

DETERMINED THAT THE lack of planning
which had caused chaos at the end of World War I would not be
repeated, the government had been preparing for peace. The first
priority was to organise the disbanding of the more than four million
service personnel, most of whom were only too ready to return home.
Housing was needed urgently. Those who could work in any aspect of
the construction industry were released first, with the proviso that,
should they leave the jobs to which they were directed, they would
be subject to recall. The order in which the remainder of the forces
would be demobbed depended on their age and length of service.
Two months' service was calculated as the equivalent of one year of
age.

A number of schemes were adopted to give the servicemen the
opportunity to find the kind of jobs they wanted. Resettlement advice
centres appeared in towns and cities across the country and proved
invaluable. Before the year was out, more than 30,000 people a week
were visiting them for advice on anything from domestic problems to
starting up a business. Millions of booklets were distributed in an effort
to make the service people's transition back to civilian life as smooth as
possible.

As each serviceman was released he was handed twelve pounds'
worth of clothing coupons and a 'demob suit'. This was partly as a
result of the protests of men like Jack Oliver, who had lost a leg at El
Alamein. He had been sent to hospital in Johannesburg and fitted with
an artificial limb before returning to England in January 1943:

I remember the day I arrived back in Britain because I arrived at Liverpool Docks, was then transported to Chester Hospital, which was some difference from the one we'd had in South Africa – food was very short; we had no sugar in our tea, I remember – and then they decided they were going to discharge us and we were sent down in an ambulance to a little old shop in Chester, one of these sort of places where farm labourers would go to be fitted out with their clothes, and we were given a pair of trousers, a coat, an overcoat, a tie and two white collars and we were told that we would come home in our khaki shirts with white collars and civvy tie, which I was most annoyed about. I made all sorts of protests but got nowhere with it at all. And also they tried to give us a cap with a button on top, which I think was about 1914–18 vintage.

I went back to my parents' house and spent a day in the pub when I first got back, everybody buying you drinks for the first couple of days and after that they forgot you were there. Most of my friends were in the forces, so I was out on a limb on my own. Anyway we coped. I remember I spent a hell of a lot of time in picture houses. My brother returned. We weren't very good friends when we were kids, but we became very good friends. We'd both grown up in the meantime.

As far as my disability was concerned, I think people were most sympathetic in the first month or two but after that, of course, it was dog eat dog. If my wife was here she'd tell you I was very bitter. I was very bitter, but not at the way we were treated by the forces; it was the way we were treated when we were given our so-called clothes, which I wouldn't have been seen dead in. In fact, one time I was up at Roehampton having a leg fitting and I was beefing on about this and a chap came to me and said, 'I'm a psychiatrist. Would you like to come and have a word with me?' So I told him about the way we were treated after we came home with this clothing business and he told me that there'd been so many complaints about this that in future people leaving the forces would be given a complete outfit, and they were.

Even so, come 1945, Ed Bruce was not happy with what the army doled out:

146

The suit looked terrible. The man that fitted me held on to a handful of excess fabric across my back so I thought it fit me when I first looked in the mirror.

Simon 'Goldie' Goldenthal had been in the army throughout the war:

I had worn army clothing consistently, including the army boots. I had never received so much as a scratch. Perhaps I dug my slit trenches deeper than most.

While I was awaiting discharge, I bought new civilian clothes, including new Oxfords. After a couple of weeks of wearing low shoes instead of boots, I noticed a red streak running up my leg. I told my girlfriend, now my wife of forty-four years, and she insisted I see a doctor. I went to Chorley Park Military Hospital and they would not let me leave. It seems I had got blood poisoning from the chafing of the shoes and, had I not gone to see about it, I might have lost my leg or even my life.

E. R. Willee had served as a naval officer during the war:

The most bizarre occurrence took place on Brighton sea-front during the evacuation of Dunkirk. I was wearing plain clothes, as I had a slight leg wound sustained during a naval assault on Zeebrugge and it was awkward getting in and out of a ratings uniform. As I sat on a bench with my wife and son, a woman stuck three white feathers on my jacket.

The demobilisation procedure worked smoothly enough, until I went to Guildford for my demob suit. A soldier took a few measurements and, without saying a word, handed me a bundle of clothes. The jacket was tight under the arms and short in the sleeves, the trousers were inches short in the leg and inches to spare in the waist. I asked if there was anything larger. The soldier said that it was the largest size he had.

Further discussion was ruled out by people behind me calling out that if we did not hurry up, they would miss their trains home. I accepted the suit with an ill grace, but took comfort from the fact that I had several pre-war suits at home and that I was slightly thinner than in 1939. I later discovered that my hopes were ill founded as the suits had been given to my brother-in-law on his return from the POW camp.

My homecoming was not greeted with much enthusiasm. My five-year-old son referred to me as 'that man'. The euphoria which had been so great at the end of hostilities had faded. Shortages of all manner of goods had caused shopkeepers to be rude to their customers. The woman at the greengrocer's said to me, 'It will do you good to get down to some work.' Service uniforms had disappeared off the streets, although many a service greatcoat had been stripped of buttons and braid and worn as civilian garments. In my visits to the local pub there was much talk of skiving and scrounging. This, I gathered, was a backlash to service discipline.

Expecting to welcome her husband on his return, Mary Scott watched a strange man heading her way:

As Ernie was due to be demobbed from R A F Cardington, I went off to meet him. I saw this vaguely familiar figure coming towards me — we've had many a laugh over it since. It was my husband! I hardly recognised him. I was so used to seeing him in uniform and he was wearing his demob suit, complete with trilby and overcoat. I thought I had met the wrong man.

Within weeks the suits could be seen everywhere. The women, obviously requiring an individual choice of clothing, were issued clothing coupons and cash to spend as they wished. Vicky Masterman was in the ATS during the war, stationed in Nottingham:

We went to Guildford to get demobbed and naturally all the men we knew were getting suits and pork-pie hats and all that sort of thing. I distinctly remember there was a suit we could take and it looked like a tweed suit with a pork-pie hat and flat shoes. But we took money and coupons so that we could buy our clothes. I don't know of any woman who took the horrible demob suits provided by the service.

Norman Worwood was a junior officer on a fleet minesweeper. He was demobbed promptly, but his homecoming was a sad one:

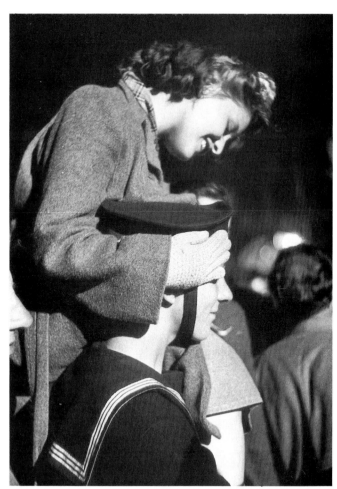

Londoners take to the
streets to celebrate VE Day,
8 May 1945.

An army car, commandeered by members of the ATS brandishing Union flags, forms part of a victory procession.

Festooned with ticker tape from neighbouring press offices, revellers dance for joy in an alley off London's Fleet Street.

Above: With his baby in tow – and the onlookers in thrall – a father pedals past the crowds gathered outside Buckingham Palace on VE Day.

Below: Canadian troops entertain Londoners in Leicester Square while they wait for the broadcast of the King's speech.

VJ Day, 15 August 1945.
Left, a jubilant American
has a bird's-eye view of
Piccadilly Circus, while
merrymakers let their
hair down in Regent
Street, below.

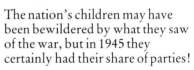

The nation's children may have been bewildered by what they saw of the war, but in 1945 they certainly had their share of parties!

A fancy-dress victory tea party for
the children of a Chelsea housing
estate.

Fraternisation in London: GIs and English girls get together in Piccadilly Circus for impromptu celebrations after the announcement of the Japanese surrender, August 1945.

Above: British women about to rejoin their GI husbands in America give their particulars to the registrar at Tidworth reception camp, near Salisbury.

Below: GI brides on their way up the gangplank of the SS *Argentina*, as they prepare to start a new life in America.

Both the German and Japanese forces had surrendered their arms and we had been engaged in clearing minefields around Burma, the Malayan archipelago and Java and, at the ripe old age of twenty-two, I had spent fifteen months abroad without any relief except the occasional shore leave and letters from home. Life aboard a small ship with a crew of less than a hundred souls can become extremely tense when such conditions prevail and all were looking forward to the day when a date for their particular demob group would be announced, when we would be assigned to another ship for passage home.

My own departure was to be much more dramatic than that! For years my father had been in indifferent health and a signal arrived at the ship's wireless office to say that he was dying and that Admiralty approval had been granted for my immediate return home for compassionate leave. Frenzied local signals passed between ship and shore and arrangements were made for me to fly forthwith from Singapore. My ship lay in Penang, some 400 miles north, and a Dakota aircraft on shuttle duties flew me to Singapore, where I boarded a converted Liberator bomber for the homeward flight. Horror and disbelief followed! The Liberator would fly only by day, making daylight stops at Penang, Rangoon, Delhi, Tel Aviv, Castelnuovo, Marseilles and, at last – hopefully! – home! Each day's flight would be merely a matter of hours, and the remainder of each day (and each night) would be spent mainly in the airfield transit huts.

Aboard the Liberator some twenty or so servicemen were flying home on compassionate grounds. During the flight, in the cramped and confined space of the stripped interior and bomb bays, we played non-stop solo whist, using our interlocked knees as a card-table until we arrived at an airfield 'somewhere in Oxfordshire'. The half-forgotten greenery of a spring day in England was a sight I shall never forget again! From the time of my leaving the ship in Penang to the landing in England it had been nine days!

After a train journey to Birmingham from Euston Station, where I had distributed single oranges and lemons (taken aboard at Tel Aviv) to delighted, but bewildered, railway staff, I arrived home. My mother was waiting at the front door. 'Pop died yesterday,' she said simply.

149

War and separation had toughened a once-shy eighteen-year-old lad, now just twenty-two, but the news was too much. I climbed the low garden fence into a field at the rear of the house garden and wept alone, tears of sorrow and frustration and weariness streaming down my face.

Many years later, my mother, who lived for forty-three years as a widow, told me that when, in 1945, I had finished my embarkation leave prior to departing for the Far East, my father had said to her as I walked off down the road, 'I shall never see him again.' For him the happy homecoming was never destined to happen and so, indeed, it proved to be.

Even for those lucky enough to survive to be reunited with loved ones, things would never be the same again. Mollie Shearing's husband, Fred, had been one of the first to be called up in 1939:

He came through the terror of Dunkirk (my thanks to God), North Africa, Italy and Austria. In February 1946 he was home for good.

By trade he was a plumber. The rule was that the firm had to take him back for at least six weeks, which they did, and then sacked him.

Joseph Haegert remembers what it was like:

I'm eighty-nine years old. I was a wireless-operator seaman during both world wars. When they came back I only heard one sentence repeated over and over: 'All we get is shit.'

John Pawling's experiences were equally demoralising:

I was at a watershed in my life after the war and I was about to go through a traumatic change: officer-paratrooper to nobody.

Tom Jones had been away from home for three years, two of them as a prisoner of war:

I was a serving policeman when the war broke out and I had a job to go back to. As a policeman with seven years' service (army service being counted in), I suffered the indignity of being placed under the wing of an older policeman for my first two weeks back on the job. My only other recollection of this time was on my first morning home I went to the local newsagent to get some papers and cigarettes and was told that they only served cigarettes to regular customers.

I. R. Dick's return was not exactly memorable:

My homecoming in 1945 was very low key. My parents had been bombed out of their flat in Clapham and had been rehoused in a flat up on Putney Heath so, on my first leave in the UK, I was met with 'Oh, it's you. Come in, then.' Not what you would call a hero's return. My father and stepmother just accepted it as another burden, I guess.

Robert Appell didn't get a hero's welcome either, when he went looking for work in London, Ontario:

The only employment I could find was as a part-time taxi driver and dispatcher. So, I applied for my own taxi licence. I appeared before the police commission, in uniform, wound stripe, ribbons and all. The police chief said he could not recommend my application because he didn't know me. I replied, 'Maybe you haven't noticed, sir. I have been away,' and left.

Edna Chambers is a rare individual. After entering the ATS in 1941, when she was twenty-four, she volunteered for duty behind enemy lines and parachuted into Bergen, Holland, to contact the underground, obtain information and return to England by fishing boat. She was sent on two of these missions:

I was back in Rugby on VE Day with my basic unit, the Heavy Artillery Records Office. I'd come down from a rest camp in North Wales – when we came back from trips behind enemy lines they put us in rest camps for a month. All the girls were going out to a dance party out at the American base. I'd just had a skin full of Americans so I said, 'OK, I'll sit in the company office and you go out. I'm not interested in the least.' I was sitting in the company office when the announcement came through that the war was over. I thought, Oh, my gosh. I just sat there. I sort of went flop, if you know what I mean. It was like somebody had pricked me and all my air had gone out.

I came out of the service in August 1945. I had none of my usual haunts to go back to. My mother had died during the war, my brother was still in India in the air force, all the girls I knew had scattered all over the country and I couldn't find any of my university pals. I felt the most lonely. I had friends but nobody who was close to me. My friends had changed drastically. They had hardened; every man for himself.

I went back to London. I wandered around sort of hopelessly. It was curious. The people who'd been home working in factories and had stayed behind had all made tremendous amounts of money and they didn't have much regard for army girls. Curious. I was made to feel like a second-class citizen and a camp follower, if you know what I mean, because I had been in the ATS. You see, they'd made pots of money and we'd been paid very little, as you know. My understanding is that the girls who went into the Auxiliary before the war were more or less slutty types, if you know what I mean. There was a sort of automatic thinking, Oh, yes, well we know your type. You're the officers' groundsheet, making your living on your back.

It was strange after leaving the ATS, having a choice of what to put on. I didn't know, besides everything I had was so darned antique.

Three weeks after that, much to my surprise, Jim arrived home and three weeks after that we got married.

Nellie Spence spent four years in the WAAF:

I was stationed in Grantham and on 22 September 1945, a group of very excited WAAFs boarded a train for Birmingham. We were so pleased to be carrying all our equipment for the last time, along with a suitcase each of civilian clothes, yet we felt a little bit of sadness at parting with good buddies.

Finally, at 4 p.m. on 23 September, I was in civilian clothes. My aunt and uncle came to meet me, as they lived in the village of Clent nearby.

The first night I had difficulty getting to sleep. The feather bed was so soft and the down quilt was a little lighter than army blankets. Also, it was so quiet. When I awoke the next morning I thought I had died and gone to heaven. All I could hear were birds singing. Then my bedroom door opened and my uncle walked in carrying a tray with a lace cloth, a red rose and my breakfast. Then I knew it was heaven on earth!

Pat Barnicott was a member of the CWAC, stationed in England during the war. This is her account of her trip back to Canada:

As we filed aboard the ship we marvelled that we were actually travelling on the gigantic *Queen 'Lizzie'*, able to carry so many troops at one time. A cabin that had once held two people was now crammed with sixteen women, four to a wall, but I did have an upper bunk. Undressing was to the accompaniment of weird animal noises that sounded like 'hubba, hubba, hubba!' originating from the dock below. So we were still women!

Fortunes were won and lost in little hidden bays aboard, where men played poker or craps. Meanwhile, I was given my birthday bumps with two husky fellows taking my arms as I hit the deck. Sometimes we clambered on piles of rafts and burst into singing *Sentimental Journey* and many of the fellows joined in.

When our great *'Lizzie'* slid gently into the harbour at New York, it was a thrill to receive such a homecoming welcome, with hooting sirens and whistling tugs all booming their greetings while cascades of water shot high into the air from other ships in the vicinity. The Liberty Lady, too, with her upraised arm, seemed to be saluting us. We crowded the rails to get our first look at the metropolis and eventually filed down the gangplank to wait to board the Hudson ferry.

We transferred to trains and all of us, servicemen and women, homeward bound at last, were naturally a bit rowdy. Not to waste another moment of this last, great adventure, groups here and there sang snatches of songs, 'rolling out the barrel' again.

Then we were on Canadian soil once more. At each station a few khaki figures lumbered off the coach after hasty don't-make-a-fuss goodbyes. With each departure the noisiness decreased, so there were little oases of silence here and there. Fatigue set in, and those not involved in card games closed their eyes. I knew there would be cousins, an aunt or two and my brother all waiting to welcome me. Would I recognise the relatives I had not seen for ten years, two years before the war had begun?

Another C W A C had just made her way down the car, obviously looking for someone, when I spotted a man in the next car dodging into the lavatory. His last words were, 'Hey, I don't want to see her now. My wife's waiting at Union Station!'

Amid the laughter that followed, a voice cried, 'It's over now, anyway.'

Yes, it was all over for all of us.

Reg Cooper had a long way to go before he was home:

Getting aboard the *Queen Elizabeth* at Southampton, 11 December 1945, I remember having a great sense of finality. I was leaving England, which had been home base for three years for me and five or six years for others. Except for the ocean being rough and watching twenty-four-hour movies sitting on both sides of the screen, the trip home was without event. I remember feeling, even then, that I was separating myself from my army buddies and thinking of myself as Reg Cooper, not Sgt Cooper G. R. At dawn on 17 December we were off Pier 59, New York City, waiting for those tugs to help us into harbour. Coming alongside we heard the strains of swing music and, looking overside, we saw dancing showgirls. The show was continuous, lasting all day. I finally got off early in the evening, only to get aboard a tender to go over to New Jersey to catch a train for Toronto. During the night we stopped in upstate New York. Getting off the train for a few minutes, I was met by an elderly couple with others handing out coffee and doughnuts – the first for years. The lady told me that she and 'Dad' met every troop train. Their boy was not coming back, and talking to us brought their son closer.

When Jack Poolton arrived back in Toronto, his father met him, and the two men made their way to northern Ontario by train:

The Ontario police had driven my mother and young brother and sister to the station before my stop to save us all meeting with a couple of hundred people that would be waiting on my home town station platform, so unbeknown to me they got them on the same train before it got to my stop. I was away washing and shaving and when I came back to the carriage they were sitting in there. It was such a shock, you know? I had made so many plans as to how we were going to meet. I had gone over it so many times while I was a prisoner. How was I going to act? Was I going to cry? Was I going to laugh? You know, you had to psych yourself up for a lot of this. You see, everybody had been so good to us since we got out of the camp, and after the treatment from the Germans. I had had chains on for 410 days, all of the Dieppe guys did. Then to be treated like kings by the Brits and Americans! Anyway, I had been preparing myself and when I met my mother I couldn't speak. It wasn't the way I'd planned it. I wasn't expecting the surprise of suddenly seeing her. I walked in with a cigarette dangling out of my mouth and my haversack over my shoulder and it was a shock. Suddenly there they were sitting there. I mean it had been five and a half years since I'd kissed her goodbye on the same station we were about to pull into.

Another Canadian, Larry MacDonald, had served in France, and recognised that he and his comrades had grown up in ways they could not have predicted:

We reached the city of Caen and Allied aircraft, American Long Toms and our own twenty-five-pounders ground the city down into rubble. Included in the rubble was one of the world's finest medieval libraries, with its priceless manuscripts and scholarly works destroyed. Whole streets had been obliterated. And after Caen the killing ground of Falaise, Canal du Nord, the Scheldt, the liberation of the Netherlands, the Hochwald and the Rhine.

And then, out of nowhere – a day in May – it was over. The silence hurt our ears. And, for the first time in a long time, one could hear the birds sing.

The war was over, not only for us, but for 45,000 Canadians who would not be going home.

Those of us who made it found, not then but later, that we had been granted some sort of a degree, a liberal arts degree from the university of the world. It came the hard way – no cap, no gown, no sheepskin. But it was there, a B A of the mind.

Now it was 'stand down' and we dispersed all across the country. 'Stay in touch, Bill.' 'You bet, Jack.' Some did; most did not.

It had been a long war. A lot had happened.

Norman C. Phemister travelled home on to a troop train from Halifax to Toronto. When the train stopped at a station along the way, he looked out the window:

We noticed a large sign: WELCOME HOME – YOU'VE DONE A GRAND JOB.

What particularly amused us was the footnote scrawled in by some wag: . . . AND NOW TRY TO FIND ONE!

Tasman Richardson's father found it difficult to settle down after five years overseas:

When he came home in the late summer of 1945 I had not seen him for nearly five years – very important years in one's life. I was asleep when he arrived in the middle of the night, having missed an earlier train from Calgary. He had been persuaded to get off there for a farewell drink with a buddy, and no doubt the civvies had kept the draught beers coming for the returning heroes. Mr Harbage, who collected the mail off the night train, deposited him at our door, and my mother said he stood there on the porch with his kit-bags, hungover and apologetic, and asked if he could come in. The steak and mushroom meal she had prepared for him had long gone cold, but I'm sure she forgave him. I know they always laughed about it in later years.

It wasn't till morning that I saw him in my mother's bed. I still remember the ambivalent feelings I had. I hadn't forgotten him, had enjoyed his letters that my mother read to me, the odd picture, the gifts at Christmas and birthdays; had prayed for his safe return and now he was here, and seemed a stranger, even an interloper into our orderly lives. I tried to identify this man, unshaven, thin, rather shy, with the jolly, loving Daddy I had kept in my memory. The Daddy who had pushed me on the swings at the playground, who had piggybacked me on climbs up Tunnel and Norquay Mountain when my little legs got tired, and had taken us on trips out west to Banff to show us where and how he was battling the pesky mosquito. (He had been foreman of the mosquito control for the parks.) The brave Daddy who had calmly turned me and my little friend Neil around and safely down the trail when a huge brown bear with cubs had suddenly confronted us, rearing up on its hind legs. The Daddy who in August of 1940 had sent me a small piece of birchbark. I still have it. On it he had written 'M.41737, Spr H. Richardson, Number 3 Company, RCETC Aug. 23, '40, Petawana, Ontario. My dear son, Not today or tomorrow, but in the years to come will the novelty of this letter be realised. Picked up along the banks of the Ottawa River – driftwood in a drifting age. Your Daddy soldiered here to stem the tide of "Hitlerism" for the cause of democracy. May God help us.'

Of course I couldn't know the ordeals he had endured; things he had seen that he never did talk about. How he might have been changed by those cataclysmic events. I knew he had been sent over two days after D-Day, had served in France, Belgium, Holland and Germany. As an engineer he hadn't been in the front lines, but had been fired upon, had a skirmish with snipers in Antwerp, had a close shave when a V1 rocket exploded taking out a block of houses right next to a canal he was guarding in Holland, but he survived the war with just a severe case of bronchitis, and an injury to his knee that later required an operation.

I realise now what a shock the return to civvy life must have been for my dad. For nearly six years he had been living with mobs of uniformed men, with air-raids, shelling, the constant tension. The relative silence now must have given him the jitters. Apparently his old job with the Parks Department wasn't available, and he seemed to be at a loose end. In a few weeks he was gone again. An old pal, Ike Mills, he met in the Legion offered him the job of cook on a two week trail ride into the mountains. They were taking out a party of wealthy Americans. I have a yellowing photo of him still wearing

his army pants, shirt and tam, tending a fire with the 'billy' boiling
near a mountain stream. He's grinning, but I remember him saying
the silence was even worse than Banff. Horseback riding was a new
experience for him, and the cayuse they gave him was not as gentle
as promised. Hell, it was his first job cooking, but I guess he bluffed
his way through and appeased the raging appetites one acquires in
that mountain air. Anyway, he did well enough that he was offered
a permanent job, but he declined. It had been a nice change, but he'd
try something else, thank you very much. He must have charmed
the Yanks with his humour and rich fund of stories as he returned
with addresses and invitations to visit them in Massachusetts. He
next picked up a job helping transport firewood or cut trees from
somewhere the other side of Lake Minnewanka. The lake was now
frozen over and they trucked them across. This proved to be as hair-
raising as the war. They would sometimes hit a bad spot and the
truck would spin wildly. Dad said he could roll a cigarette and half
smoke it before they came to a stop and could proceed. The
knowledge that a D-Cat and drive had gone through the ice never to
be seen again, a year or two before, did not help my dad's nerves. I
think he stuck it out till the first pay cheque. Said he would rather
face Jerry's bombs!

*Doreen Barnley was very close to her brother Victor and one day, out
of the blue, she received a phone call at her place of work in Rosebery
Avenue, London:*

Victor was phoning from Kings Cross. He was on his way to his
army camp, where he would get a leave pass. I raced to my boss's
office to ask permission to go to Kings Cross, pelted down to
Farringdon Road, jumped on a moving bus and raced into Kings
Cross station. It was crowded with forces. I ran along, asking
anyone who looked my way, 'Do you know Vic Barnley?' You can
guess the cheeky answers. They were all so pleased and excited to be
home. I looked in the offices and canteen and, unbelievably, I
spotted him in the telegraph office or such. I threw the door open
and got swung off my feet like I was still his kid sister. He told me at
a later date I had sent his mate flying who was behind the door.

I think we had three reunion parties. After all that excitement we expected things to begin to get back to some normality. But the rationing still continued and for those, like two of my brothers, who married in the war, there were no houses or flats, or for myself, when I married my air force gunner a year later. 'Homes for Heroes' we were promised in the war. That was a laugh and a half.

I can't say my sisters-in-law were upset at giving up their work. They had worked hard, especially Nellie – twelve hours a day for six and seven days a week. I came into the country to my husband's home, to live with his mother. My husband was demobbed in January 1947. We spent my husband's demob money doing up two rooms in the village – we had eight years there – a bucket lavatory and water from a pump in the street. My children were born there. We had mostly second-hand furniture, as that was rationed by dockets. It was a struggle and we eventually built ourselves a bungalow which we still occupy. I suppose we stuck it out as we thought ourselves the fortunate ones. My brothers came back and we had survived (just). I have only one brother left now. I think the war shortened their lives. We won the war, but at what cost?

Marigold Hoare was a WRN and had served in Ceylon for eighteen months. After her wartime experiences she found her new outlook on life varied considerably from what her parents expected of her:

We docked at Liverpool to a band playing. Down there was my mother and, well, she didn't recognise me at first because my hair was absolutely bleached from the sun.

Then she said, 'Could I possible have something to eat?' I got her some rolls off the ship and she hadn't seen white bread since the war had started, but coming from Ceylon, no rationing or anything, we had beautiful white rolls.

It was an enormous disappointment because, you realise, we'd got away from wartime England and our families – and life in those days for young people was very restricted – and we'd been living a totally independent and marvellous life in the Far East, very spoiled, with very few WRNS and lots of glamorous parties, given by officers on ships and so on. For instance, there was no clothes rationing in Ceylon, obviously, and you could go into a shop and buy silk to have dresses made and, of course, all that marvellous sun and climate.

We came back to a grey England, still in the grips of austerity and back again into a very restrictive home life. Our parents had been quite unable to understand the changes that had happened and, of course, the 1939–45 war was a very great upheaval of social life, and life in general, and things were no longer the same for people who'd managed to get away or get out in the world, you know. And they came back and, of course, their parents expected them to fall back into a slot. I had extreme difficulty in getting my father to agree to let me go on working. He thought one's bit for the war had been done and one would return to living the life of leisure and good works down in the country. And, of course, we thought very differently and I say 'we' because I know this happened to a number of my friends.

Almost the very first thing I did much to my parents' disappointment – but they didn't actually try to stop me – was I tried to find another job that would take me overseas. I almost got signed up to go to Malaya. I was asked what my parents would think about my doing this and, being a fairly honest, truthful young thing, I said they would be extremely unhappy. So, they said, in that case, we're terribly sorry, we can't take you.

In Gloucester there wasn't any petrol, I remember, so you didn't go to many parties. Clothes rationing was still on. It was pretty austerity-ridden, after this wonderful year and a half, when one had seen a totally different kind of life overseas, because Ceylon was comparatively untouched by the war. There were plenty of civilian people living there, planters and so on, whose lives were absolutely the same. It hadn't changed at all. The social life was still in full swing, you'd never know there'd been a war on. No problems in that direction, so you can imagine what England was like when we came back. I'm sure we were a very unsettling influence on the home and it must have been very difficult for our parents to still accept us.

I, a girl, was expected to return to the same sort of semi-dutiful life that the other people lived in. I don't think that our parents' attitude grew with the war; ours had totally changed and I found that life was very boring. I remember one friend of mine who, just before the war, had signed up to become a companion to an old lady down in the country somewhere. The war came and saved her and she joined the ATS and had the most marvellously exciting time.

But, you see, opportunities like that in one sense opened up a world which was completely closed to a lot of people. I think it set one on an independent course. I later insisted on going to London and taking a typing course which, out of interest, my father refused to pay for. He refused to give me any money to further my studies because I was supposed to have finished with all that, you see, and stay at home. But I got the WRNS to pay for that. I got a grant and I took a six-week typing course and was thus able to find a secretarial job and earn a perfectly good living ever since.

My mother, in particular, had a really dreary war, staying at home, coping with family, trying to feed them, doing all the local war work, which wasn't very glamorous, you know. It would have been less than human, if they hadn't been – my mother anyway – very slightly envious. Not that the WRNS was entirely glamorous, there was the other side to it which was very hard work and, when it was in England, a lot of it very boring. But we'd had a rather glamorous war with lots of friends, we'd been able to get out and about, we'd seen an interesting part of the world that normally one wouldn't have been able to see, and I think, frankly, that they were a little bit envious.

It must have been very difficult for them to accept us in a more independent role. We'd grown up, I suppose, in a way in which they couldn't imagine. In those days I was twenty-one. I'd totally changed in their eyes. I'd met people that normally I'd never had a chance of meeting, from all different backgrounds. I'd lived with them, I'd done things, I'd seen things. I was far advanced of what their idea of a daughter of twenty-one perhaps had been. I don't think it was anybody's fault; it was inevitable that this difference would have taken place.

The slight clash came with my parents in silly things, like we'd been used to running our own lives completely, wearing what we wanted to wear, all those small things which, in those days, was subject to pretty heavy criticism or importance by one's parents. But then, at least from the background I came from, it was very heavily controlled, you know. And, of course, it just didn't work any more because one wasn't prepared to put up with that.

I've since talked to many other people about my age and it is fairly prevalent among my friends that they did find life very restrictive after being in the services, both men and women, and in particular those of us who had been overseas. And there was the chance to meet other people because England before the war was divided into such rigid compartments and you hardly ever stepped out of one into the others. But, during the war, all that ended and one had a much more interesting life, in many ways. Women no longer remained stuck in the kitchen with their sole duty to the home. They were, even with doing boring war work at home, able to get out and find a freedom they'd never had before.

When the future Mrs Pat Moore joined the WAAF in 1940, she was engaged to be married to a farmer:

In my case the position was reversed. As you know, farming was a reserved occupation and farmers were urgently needed on the home front. So I went off to war and my fiancé was left behind to fight his own battles on the home front.

I served with about six other WAAFs and a hundred or more airmen so I'm sure the girls got rather spoiled, as the airmen competed for our favours (of an innocent nature), although, to my credit, I remained faithful to my farmer. We were married one fine day in July 1942 and, after three days' honeymoon, I returned to my unit. Most of the airmen became even more protective, warding off the good-time Johnnies who thought a separated bride might be easy game. A year or so later I became pregnant and was duly released from service.

Coming back to Civvy Street was not easy. I missed the companionship, the demanding work and, of course, the discipline. My husband was still working very long hours and I'm sure never saw our baby daughter awake until she was several months old. I did not come from farming stock so had to learn to cope with poultry, the lambing and looking after the small creatures, plus feeding the hordes of people on meagre rations all became my life.

We have retired from farming now and, upon reflection, there is very little I would have changed, most certainly not my service days and the many friends I made. I don't think I would have coped so well if the roles had been reversed.

In common with other service personnel, Bill Lancaster found it hard to readjust:

Civvy life after six years in the service was very traumatic for me. There was no apparent reason and I counted my blessings that I had 'come out of it', including many of the major campaigns and invasions, etc., virtually unscathed. Settling down seemed to be almost impossible and I tried several different jobs – fire service, post office, plumbing and factory work – but it was all so different from the army and driving lorries, coaches and motorbikes, etc. Eventually, I obtained an introduction and interview for the *Daily Mail*. I remained in Fleet Street for the rest of my working life.

Elsie Brackenborough's fiancé came out of the RAF, where he was a wireless-operator air-gunner with a good rank. They were married in 1946:

In the first five years of our marriage my husband had thirty-five jobs, all because he was a government-trained plasterer.

These problems were not confined to Britain. Frank O'Connor, known as Okie or Blackie, was from Canada, and his return home was no easier:

Having served in the navy for over five years, war's end found me in the Irish Sea, heading for Newfoundland. We left Ireland at 4 a.m. and the war was over at 8 a.m. Consequently, we were unable to celebrate since, as far as our ship's crew was concerned, we were still at war and had to act accordingly. The possibility of German submarines still on duty was certainly a reality. Nevertheless, we were promised to splice the main brace (receive an extra drink of rum) on our arrival in Newfoundland. Needless to say, forty-five years later we are still waiting for that to happen.

The feelings of the crew at war's end were mixed feelings, of course. It was a joyous relief to know that war was over. On the other hand, parting each other's company had an aspect of sadness. Can you imagine having been taught to kill or be killed for five years then, overnight, all this is brought to a sudden halt?

Well, returning to Canada was being completely disoriented. It was really a time of complete discontentment. How does one help to fight a war for five years then try to fit into a civilian job if there was a job to have? Trying to find a satisfactory job was, to me, the most difficult part of adjusting to Civvy Street. Secondly, having lived and worked in a navy uniform, I found it difficult to return to civvy clothing.

For about a year later I found I drowned my problems with alcohol. Soon I discovered that didn't help matters, so packed that up once and for all.

Roy Nethercott had joined the Royal Navy in 1942 at the age of eighteen, having volunteered when he was seventeen.

I was demobilised in 1946. I had seen service in North Africa, Sicily and Europe. I was a 'khaki' soldier, serving as a landing-craft coxswain, beach commando and, finally, as an underwater-demolition and military bomb-disposal person.

I was one of those who were swept up in the demobilisation fever. A new suit, a funny hat and no one to boss me about.

After the first excitement of being home came the moment of truth. I woke up one day and looked into the future and saw . . . nothing. For the first time in five years I was on my own, no comrades, no system to support me. I felt worse than I did when I sat on top of a 200-pound bomb. At least then I had been trained to deal with that risk. My mother wanted me to be the little boy who went to war, my former girl wanted me to be her security blanket.

For some who were accustomed to the service life with its discipline and regulated days, the boredom of staying home and searching the papers for a job became insufferable. One woman remembers:

Men were returning to Civvy Street and coming out of the services without jobs to go to, and this was to cause problems. My father had been a regular airman, and for him to be demobbed was a very traumatic experience. He did not know what to do with himself. He moped about the house, became ill, and was dead within two years.

Horace Neame left in 1941, when his baby son was just five months old; he did not get home again until 1946:

164

I couldn't settle down for some time after I came back. I was so used to being with men, no children. I was pleased when I could go to work and get with the men for a while.

My son was really upset about me being there. He didn't want me at all. It took some time. Every time I looked at him or got near him he used to cry. The only time I was happy was when I was at work with the chaps.

James Sims had been a POW in Germany and was back in England in a hospital when the war ended:

I was sort of prostrate, you know. My legs kept going until I landed on English soil and then I collapsed. I was down to just under seven stone. In eight months I went from eleven stone seven to just under seven stone. It was only just willpower that kept me going, I think really.

I remember the flight back to England vividly. I can't remember the exact day. It was a fantastic feeling. A lot of the older men cried when they saw the white cliffs of Dover. They'd been prisoners for five years, since Dunkirk, and it was too much for them, you know. It was a very emotional moment.

Some were apprehensive about going home. I didn't really feel that way. I mean your family welcomed you back. But there was that apprehension, especially with the men who had been prisoners a long time of how they would settle down again with their wives. There were a lot of cases, of course, where the wives had gone off with other men.

A chap in our ward of Ashridge House – he was an ex-prisoner of the Japanese – he was in such a state, I hated to go near his bed, you know. He was like a living skeleton. His sister arrived to see him and she couldn't wait to tell him his wife had left him for another man. He collapsed and, of course, the nursing sister was furious. But these infidelities weren't as widespread as I think they would have been these days. People weren't so obsessed with sex in those days.

I was lucky. My family were wonderful. Of course, they were so relieved to see me and I was an only child. I was shocked by my mother's appearance because she had aged terribly with the strain, I think, and that gave me quite a turn when I saw her and realised what an upset I'd put them to. Mind you, they were upset at my appearance, too. I was a sort of yellow, sickly colour, you know.

One mistake a lot of people made was trying to feed you up, give you great meals. Of course, your stomach couldn't take them. We had quite a few ex-prisoners die as a result of this. They gave warnings at the hospitals, but if a man didn't go to hospital and went straight home quite a lot of them died from eating too much. The food was too rich, you see, and your stomach had shrunk and that was it, you couldn't deal with it. All I could do was to push the plate aside and say, 'I'm sorry, I just can't eat all that.' I actually ate fertiliser when I was a prisoner. I didn't know it was fertiliser but when you're that hungry you'll eat anything. So, it was strange to refuse food once I was home. We used to say when we were prisoners that we would never refuse anything ever again, but we did, of course, because you had to.

It was difficult to adjust to being home again. Not mentally, but physically I had a lot of trouble, with the malnutrition and a leg wound. I was in and out of different military hospitals.

Despite the problems facing those who returned with a physical disability, their plight was much less than that of similar victims of World War I. The memory of some of those veterans, forced to beg on street corners, helped ensure that servicemen injured in World War II were better cared for. Even so, treatment was primitive by today's standards.

Charles Dunham returned home in 1942 after losing a leg in North Africa in 1941. He is a past general secretary of the British Limbless Ex-Servicemen's Association (BLESMA) and at the end of the war was very involved in the welfare of the disabled.

The problem was getting used to disability, in that there was, at that time, very little physical rehabilitation. You were fitted with a limb, you walked around a limb centre for ten minutes and then you were sent home with it and you did the best you could.

We came into Glasgow on a boat from South Africa. We were sent home from the hospital eventually without being fitted with artificial limbs, on crutches. We were given an escort to get across to the mainline station in Edinburgh from Glasgow but then we were on our own, with crutches and kit-bags. I finished up on Peter-borough Station in the early hours one morning in 1942, waiting for the paper train to go up to my home, which was near Spalding. And an air-raid alarm was on. That's the way we were looked after in those days. We were discharged before being fitted with artificial limbs.

When I finally arrived home it was pretty weepy, I suppose. You've come back from the dead and you're disabled, you know. It is a shock, not only for the individual himself that is disabled in service, but it's also a shock for his family. There was no friction, no friction at all, but in some cases life was a bit difficult. If a man had been wounded and lost a leg in, say the Far East and been a Jap POW for about five years before being eventually repatriated after the end of the Second World War, he very often came home to a whole mess of domestic problems. You know, he came home to find somebody else living with his wife, and all that business. This is what goes on, it's human nature, but it makes life very difficult.

As to the various reactions of people, well, if the injury is obvious you're all right, but in the case of an artificial limb, you see, you can wear an artificial limb and, apart from a slight limp when you walk, there is no obvious disability. So, you were a young man, in the eyes of the world fairly fit and active, not in service and this could often present problems by people who would tell you you ought to be in the bloody army. That wasn't so easy. The funny thing is that when the war ended I don't think I felt anything. I think most people were very excited and happy but, if you're starting out on a new life with severe disablement, you were a bit skeptical or suspicious of what life is likely to be long term.

John Donovan had joined the Territorial Army and went to Singapore with his division. He was taken prisoner by the Japanese, went to work on the River Kwai, and developed a tropical ulcer on his leg. His leg was taken off in the jungle by an Australian surgeon in November 1943. He remained a prisoner for a further twenty-two months, and during that time heard the news that the war was over:

The guards seemed to disappear and there was quietness for a while and then finally in the evening – we were in a massive camp for the disabled and people who were no longer working – and we were given this announcement that the war was over in the evening of that day. I remember I had dengue fever at the time and so went out there looking like grim death. But I do remember then obviously cheering and the singing. We had, of course, Australians, British, Dutch with us, a mixture, and we sang national anthems, I think, and probably one hymn. This was all spontaneous from people on crutches, with every disease under the sun, we all came together in this big hut of this camp in Thailand, which was this post-railway hospital camp for what you might call the permanently sick. There were thousands there. We were so relieved.

I remember arriving back in England, excitement mixed with apprehension. It all went so very quickly. I arrived in Euston late in the evening, dark, that's where the crowds were, not Liverpool. That's where we suddenly lost touch with one another because we'd been together with our friends since we boarded the ship in the Far East. Then suddenly you disgorge in Euston into this mass of people, and wonder what on earth is happening, and suddenly I heard somebody coming along shouting my name and a strange man came up to me and he said, 'I'm from the Kent Red Cross and I've got a car here for you and I'm taking you home.' And he said, 'Where's your kit?' so I pointed and I had by then accumulated two kit-bags nearly as tall as he was, because when you've been a prisoner of war you keep anything, anything you're given you take. I remember he picked one up to swing it and it nearly swung him!

I'm now by myself in the back of a car, coming through London and wondering what it's all about with the lights. We get to Chislehurst and we turn the corner and my house was floodlit, with an American flag almost as big as the house, and all sorts of other flags. I gathered that during the course of the years, being missing, my parents had been in touch not only with the British but the American set-up to see if they could get any information. Anyway, they'd borrowed a flag from the American Embassy. I remember going inside the house, sitting down – I've lost my crutches by now, so I'm sitting down – and being kissed by one lady after another. God knows who they were! Half of Chislehurst, I should think! After that, the other memory that sticks is going to bed and being unable to move with all the blankets being put on me.

I think then, and the feeling could be expressed today, I think my friends and I use the phrase 'life everyday has been a bonus since then' because we never expected to come back. That's why I don't complain to this day no matter what happens because, well, I've looked upon it as a bonus. Some prisoners may have been apprehensive but I wasn't. When you got back home there was so much love – I can say this now, my beloved parents are dead – there was so much love that you were swallowed at the beginning, you know, loads of blankets tucking you in so that you could hardly move. That, combined with you'd suddenly lost everybody you'd depended on for a long time, you were surrounded by love, but it was a different kind of love.

I had nearly a year off. That was the saving, in a sense, because I thought out what I wanted to do for the future, my profession. I decided I wanted to teach and later on went to college and picked it all up again and lived happily ever after, except for the things that have happened to all of us.

The wonderful thing was that there was no strain with my parents. They were terribly shocked, obviously emotionally upset but, as anyone who knew about the Japanese prisoner-of-war camps, they were so relieved that you were coming back. The bits that were missing (my leg) didn't matter much. They wanted, obviously, to overdo the looking after you and it took time, so there is a strain. I found at the beginning there was a loneliness and you found yourself sitting in the local pub, but you found there was nobody there to talk to. The young people set up a local club which one went to and I was fortunate enough to meet my future wife. You waited six months to get your artificial limb and so your life was very much tied up with how you could manage on this thing that always seemed three inches too long. I've had some hard knocks since, nevertheless I'm very grateful that I'm still here. Some of my buddies felt resentment about the war, especially toward the Japanese but, if you take up a career of teaching the next generation, one thing you don't teach is hate.

I occasionally had dreams in the early days. It definitely leaves doubts for a time. It takes time to be back again. And, of course, you'd go along to a bus and it would disappear out of your hand as you'd put your hand out to get it because of my disability. Life had

169

its problems to start with, and who could you talk with that could really understand? People were kind. You were very receptive to kindness anyway, because there had been the feeling with the Japanese all along that you are always wary, at the very least, and anything could happen and often did. So, getting back again and being able to do what you liked, amongst people who, although they didn't know you, there was no unkindness.

I received especially kind treatment while I was still on crutches and was in uniform. Later, after getting an artificial limb and being able to walk on it quite well, no one could tell I was disabled and so I was treated like everyone else. That was a bit difficult to get used to as I was still disabled.

Canadian Wilf Jones was nineteen when he went overseas and was away for four birthdays. He served in England and Normandy as a troop sergeant, losing his leg near Caen:

I was flown back to England with a bunch of English soldiers. Don't ask me how I got in there; I'll never know. I wound up in the children's ward in Radcliffe Infirmary, Oxford. I can remember coming to and wondering what all these queer things were and it was Snow White and the Seven Dwarfs painted on the wall! I wondered where I was.

I arrived back in Canada on 9 December 1944. I came back on the hospital ship *Lutecia*. That was her first run with wounded on board. We left Liverpool and we went down by the Azores and the Canaries and across Bermuda and into Halifax. We were treated very well on board. The white bread was excellent. It was their first trip across and the staff weren't used to English money, which was what we had. And, of course, on the ship were Canadians who had come up from Italy and were being evacuated to Canada. So, for the first couple of days we paid the ship's staff off in sixpences and francs and God knows what and they were losing money on us and so they paid us off in Canadian money. We were treated well. It was a good ship.

It was a long voyage because it was a Red Cross ship and it had those arms out the side with floodlights on, shining on the red cross. The first night out everybody said, 'Oh, my God, this ship's all lit up!' You know England was all blacked out.

When we got to Halifax the main thing, I think, in everybody's minds was to get leave to go home. I was a stretcher case but I had been up on crutches quite a bit and, when I got on the train, one of the officers asked me, 'Are you mobile?' I said, 'I'm very mobile,' because I was thinking of leave, you know. When I got on the train I found out they had given me a top bunk! I remember very well that it was a Red Cross train but it had civilian employees on it. We had a porter and any time I wanted to get in the bunk he had to give me a boost up. I remember when we had our first meal the train still had the white tablecloths, silverware, bread and butter, which in itself was quite a treat. And we had cream on the ship, too.

The train took me to Toronto. On the ship, because I lived in Peterborough, my depot was Kingston and somebody came around and said, 'Do you want to change depots?' There were people changing depots from Montreal to some place out west or wherever. So I changed mine to Toronto. We came into Toronto and they took us to Chorley Park.

All I had was a small haversack and I had a big stuffed animal that I'd made in therapy. My brother met me in the Exhibition Grounds; he'd been discharged ahead of me, and then we went to Chorley Park. I remember the ambulance broke down on the way to Chorley Park. I had been knocking around with three other amputees and when we were in the ambulance in England to go to the ship, it broke down!

In those days you took the bus to Port Hope and changed buses. When I got to Port Hope and looked out the window, I saw another brother and my girlfriend and her father. They had phoned all around and I guess they had told them at Chorley Park that I was on that bus, so I came the rest of the way to Peterborough by car.

I hadn't seen my girlfriend since February 1941. I remember when we rolled into the Toronto station, as I said there were three of us amputees that knocked around together, and the fellow from Toronto said, 'If my mother starts to cry I'm going to buzz off.' We said, 'Don't be crazy because she'll just be glad to see you.' But there was a certain amount of apprehension.

When I got home they had a big sign across the street, which kind of threw me because I didn't expect that. In fact I think I kind of hurt my dad's feelings because I was only in there about ten minutes and

I said, 'Dad, will you get that sign down?' It said 'Welcome home, Wilf.' It came down right away.

It never seemed to be hard for my girlfriend. The only thing that I noticed that was different was that we were both smoking now! I didn't really notice that much different. We carried on where we left off and were married in three weeks.

When I had written home to say that I had lost my leg, my fiancée went out and got her operator's licence so that she could drive me around because I couldn't drive; there were no automatics in those days. I didn't have enough money to buy a car anyhow.

When I got back to Toronto from leave with my wife, the news had come across that the peace had been signed. Well, there was nothing for me to do but to get on one of the old streetcars and rattle off to Christie Street Hospital. Then when I got there, the nurse said, 'What are you doing here?' Everyone had just taken off, left, right and centre.

A few of us sat there and talked. It was kind of a funny feeling. To be honest with you, up to that time the war was still on and we were wounded but we were kind of thankful to be out of it, out of it alive. But then, all of a sudden it's over and you realise that you're going to have a tough row to hoe for a while.

I've been married for forty-six years now, with three children and eight grandchildren.

Daisy Howell had been married during the war. Her husband arrived home after losing a leg in combat:

My father used to lift him in and out of his wheelchair and lift him into bed, that's how we managed. They sent him home from Roehampton with a peg leg and as much as said, 'Well, try and walk' and that's how it was. He was very cheerful. He took it very well and he didn't hold any animosity towards the Germans. He said they were doing their job the same way that he was doing his, and he was quite philosophical about it, really. He made a lot of nice German friends and they used to write to each other. My father used to carry him about because he was very thin then and his remaining leg was in plaster up to his thigh. He had more trouble with the leg they saved than the one he lost.

172

The initial feeling of excitement at the prospect of peace and prosperity soon gave way to dejection as returning servicemen and women looking forward to a land of plenty instead faced post-war cutbacks. There was a shortage of meat in Britain; the bacon ration of four ounces was cut to three after the victory. The clothing ration was also cut, as a shortage of labour in the mills forced a reduction in the production of textiles. But housing remained the most serious problem.

Toni Daly was a corporal in the ATS and worked as a clerk in London. She felt quite lost:

I had just got engaged about that time but we hadn't got any money to buy a home, so we lived with my parents when we got married. We thought it would only be for a year but it ended up to be nine years. They were hard years because my husband was quarrelling with my mother. They were both good people, but they just couldn't live together. So I was like a referee, really, for nine years until we got our own home. Most of the young people I knew were in the same position, so most of us went to live with our relatives and that led to quite a lot of troubles, especially if you had young children.

I didn't feel any resentment that the hardships seemed to be continuing after the war was won. I felt that the war was forced on us and we'd all fought it in our own way and we'd all got to adjust together. We were so busy trying to make a little life for ourselves that we were practical – we were lucky to be alive.

In my case, my having been a corporal in the army made it a little difficult for my husband. I think he wanted to be in charge of things. But, of course, living with my parents, as you can imagine, didn't please my mother who also liked to be in charge of everything and she had every right to be because it was her house. I was a referee.

We didn't really go out at all and when we bought our house it was even worse because we couldn't afford to go out or have a drink or do anything because we were struggling so hard to pay the mortgage. We shouldn't have got married then. We should have saved until we could get a home, but then my husband wanted to get away from his parents. My husband was one of seven children and he was a sergeant and two of his brothers were officers, and all these boys were coming home to a three-bedroom semi-detached house and they'd been men in charge of other men, you see. They felt they just couldn't stand Mum treating them as her little boys.

For Marcia Vardon the war had acted as a great leveller. She hoped that in the new world order, class and background would never be as important again:

Demobbing of the troops began but it was spread over a long period and the return of men in their ill-fitting new suits and raincoats sometimes brought shocks and disappointments, as well as rejoicing. I had been writing for years to a soldier I had only known briefly before his call-up. He came back with serious hopes and intentions, which a very short time in his company made me realise were not for me to share, and a difficult time ensued to convince him of this.

The New Look, which soon became fashion, cheered us up, as the longer and more fancy dresses and skirts became available after so many years of scrimping, altering and making do. Rationing, though, continued for several years: tea not being freed until October 1952, sugar in 1953, and butter, margarine and cheese in 1954. Fresh fruit gradually reappeared in the shops and there were many children who saw bananas for the first time and didn't know how to tackle them.

The special government departments set up to cope with wartime emergencies – fuel, food, labour, etc. – gradually came to an end and, as rebuilding took place, first with temporary huts, etc., then with fine new buildings, the big residential houses were returned to their owners or became flats for the new generation of young people. Looking back now, it probably took as many years for life to settle down again as the whole war had lasted, but for most of us it was a slow, gradual development with new relationships and new families being born to grow up with World War II as part of their history.

But demobilisation did not bring Edna Bucknill's husband home. As a war widow, she had to learn to cope with a very different world:

I was aware of a long period of greyness following the war. In spite of the relief there was an anticlimax, a feeling of pricked-balloon deflation in the period of May to August 1945.

Kindness seemed to have disappeared. Pre-war morals seemed to have disappeared along with good manners. Queues were no longer orderly and people became insular all over again.

Men coming home found homes that were very shabby and often overcrowded – if they had a home still – in the grey apathy and chill that seemed to pervade for several years. Sometimes getting food seemed worse than the war years, as rationing continued for so long. The black marketeers were still flourishing and bartering was as rife here in Great Britain, particularly London, as it had ever been.

Many wartime marriages suffered defeat. There was no more excitement, you see. Even those whose bonding had a pre-war basis had, in those years after the war, so many difficulties to surmount. Many had come home to children they didn't know and the children objected to the newcomer. They found wives who were no longer the quiet, simple shop assistant or office clerk, but women who had become sophisticated in all manner of ways, who could cope with all manner of things and had begun to want more than their mothers had. These men missed their pals. They were now alone with responsibilities they'd never had before.

As a young war widow, I was among the ranks of 'the walking wounded'. Almost ignored, as if one had a dread disease that no one wanted to know about. War widows were disregarded. You couldn't get accommodation easily. WW Pensions were treated as 'unearned income' for tax purposes and, therefore, taxed at the highest rate possible. How about that for losing my husband, three brothers, my home and a baby?

Everything you can name was very slow to become available, even with dockets for utility furnishings. Commodities of all kinds were a long while becoming available because of shortages. No longer were you treated to 'Don't you know there's a war on?' but to insolence, arrogance and sniggers. Bartering was in all things and, if you had nothing to barter with, you went without. World War II and its after-years destroyed kindness and good manners forever.

I well remember the prop – a wooden pole for holding up a clothes line, which I think saved my sanity. As I have said, I was a young and very broken war widow and was living with my mother. We were frozen, like everyone else. No coal had come for weeks and in a tiny room with a Scrooge-like fire in a tiny grate, we had burned all we could think of to keep a modicum of warmth to heat the little kettle on a trivet and ourselves – when she remembered the clothes prop. We could not saw it up, so it was placed across the landing into the room and into the grate. It was slowly fed through the bars as it burned. The kettle boiled and a joyous evening resulted, the prop keeping us warm for about two and a half hours. Can you imagine inching the long prop through the door and across the room? It was hilarious. My younger brother, aged about twelve, was the official threader. The laughter warmed us too, for there had been little of that for a very long time.

After serving three years in the ATS, Olive Perry was pregnant with her first child. She was demobbed in 1945 and went to join her husband Brian in Swindon, Wiltshire, where he was serving with the National Fire Service:

It was a strange town to me, as I was a Bristolian and wanted to return to Bristol. We found a small bedsitting room in a house rented by Londoners who had come to Swindon to get away from the raids. My baby was born in Swindon Maternity Home in December of that year.

One day we were told that a lot of people were moving into old army camps outside Swindon. Anything was better than being in rooms. The camp was nearly full. The only empty hut was the cookhouse, with the large range taking up most of the room. We lit the range to boil a kettle with some wood and we became squatters.

We had many privations. There were many ex-servicemen and women whose only hopes were to be rehoused in the future, but some couldn't stand the camp life and went to live with relatives. The local council took over the camp and put in electric meters, running water and made the huts waterproof. The rent was eleven shillings a week. After two years in the cookhouse hut, we moved into a better hut with small rooms which had been the guard room.

It even had a bath, but no hot water. Brian made me a strong iron stand to place over the primus stove so I was able to heat a bucket of water.

Joyce Bayley had also been in the ATS; she was demobbed in October 1947 and went back home to live in London. It was not a happy experience:

Having spent the last eighteen months of service life in Brecon, South Wales, it was quite a shock trying adjust to Civvy Street.

I left the barracks in Aldershot, a demobilisation centre, on 7 October, with an amount of cash, clothing coupons, a travel warrant designated to a place of your choice within Great Britain, and a month's leave! That was it, you were on your way! No more daily or part-one orders to be read and digested, no more lining up to salute for your pay each week, no more being on parade or kit inspections or FFIs. The ordered, comradely days were over!

My money and clothing coupons were spent on smart clothes in order to go searching for a job to re-establish myself in civilian life.

Whilst away, my mother had moved house twice so it was to a new district that I went and, because of the war, some friends had lost their lives, others had been bombed out so had moved away. Some, like me, were still in the services awaiting their termination of duties.

What I could not get used to was being in London! It was big, dirty and noisy. At that time there was no Clean Air Act in force and during the 1947–48 winter we had nasty fogs, 'pea-soupers' as they were called. I hated it.

Violet Kirkwood found that life had changed after the war with men who had been demobbed wandering about, at a loss to know what to do with themselves:

The home life had gone. Men from the forces did not think for themselves any more. Money was just spent and spent on anything they wanted. My husband took out various girls. I was his mother, not his wife. I found this out when he had a birthday card from one of his girlfriends. I also got chocolates from her to his mother (me)

177

when he came home on leave. He could not see how wrong it was.

I had to work to keep the place going, but was still expected to pay all bills: electric, mortgage, phone, food, etc. He even said my daughter was not his child. Then, as she grew older, he landed others for a baby but showed his own pretty daughter off. He would walk on the other side of the road in order not to talk to me. I was too staid for him. He wanted life and sex, not worrying who paid for it.

War made some men. Some did not even bother to grow up. They did not like taking orders, so got the rotten jobs of toilet cleaners and potato bashing. My husband had been born fairly well off, with servants, but could not take command or give orders, so he was very fed up all the time and took it out on us at home.

Jobs were hard to get and money tight. The men who went as objectors and refused to fight came off best. They kept the best jobs, had good money and food, plus a good home life, the whole of the war and after the war they kept their jobs. The servicemen were degraded again and put at the odd jobs, when before the war they had been the top men with good money.

Women also kept working, keeping men out of jobs which they knew they could do. A lot of men could not understand why the women had to work once they were home again. Barriers were put up between men and women.

May Wilson was waiting to be invalided out of the services:

The day peace broke out (with apologies to the old-time comedian Robb Wilton), I was on an RAF camp, somewhere in England, a cog and a small part of the Number 26 Bomber Group. I had served as a WAAF for three years. I was no longer up to the medical standard required by the force. I was nearly twenty-one years of age! My health had deteriorated and I had undergone major surgery.

Although I had looked forward to the end of the war, as we all had done, and VE and VJ days had brought great celebrations amongst all on our camp, I felt so sad I was going to have to leave the great companions I had made. The comradeship amongst us all during the war period had been quite unique and wonderful. The future for our country and our Allies seemed very hopeful to us, and we had been promised the usual 'land fit for heroes' to which we could return. I was going to be able to vote for the very first time in my life; this was a very sobering thought. As I wasn't a heroine, and my life in the service had been of a quiet, clerical nature, the reflected glory from brave deeds of others and their 'winning the war' was something which I had enjoyed. Doing 'my bit', as it was called then, had somehow helped the heroes and heroines to win the war.

So, off I went home to Bootle on sick leave and then to Civvy Street after three months' paid leave. The future was a mystery and a challenge. The home I returned to was strange because I had to fit into it again. I missed my service life and the routine, and home was not so welcoming as I had thought it would be. There were no banners up saying 'Welcome Home', and perhaps I had expected something along those lines. It seemed just like going back home from a holiday or a spell of leave, and it didn't seem final.

I felt very lonely and alone and somehow in the way of the routine of the house. I wandered around amongst old haunts and looked up friends I had known but, after a few weeks, this began to create a need within me to find another style of life, a life with purpose, with a goal of some sort at which to aim. I had entered the war effort as a happy young girl volunteer for my country and had been happy to go, but I left the war behind at the end of the service life as a very serious-thinking and questioning young woman, questioning all the future plans our politicians were promising us.

I was beginning to realise that this service life had taken the place of the other life I might have been living, and I wondered what it would have been like. Would I have been a different person now if I'd been allowed to spend them at college and gone on to a career or married a local lad and followed the course of my mother?

My parents needed money to aid the housekeeping bills in order to keep me and so I had to find a job. My old bedroom had been given to someone else and my civilian togs had been given in exchange for clothing coupons by my mother, and so I didn't have very much in material wealth!

Although we had known some hard times in the WAAF, we had

also known such friendship, and now I was extremely lonely and alone and felt bereft, as if I had suffered a death within me. I saw the men around the camps getting ready to join the breadwinner trail again and we, as servicewomen, all talked about our roles in the 'new world fit for heroes' and wondered about where we would fit in as 'the heroines'. We were not 'persons' yet, but still a number, rank and name, and we had to try to forget the past now and start all over again.

The night before I actually left the RAF hospital at Ely, Cambridgeshire, the gang had arranged for us to attend a dance in Cambridge given by the RAFA, and it was to be my grand farewell and my send off to Civvy Street. Whilst there at the function, as I was unable to dance, I was given the task of selling the raffle tickets at the door and it was there I saw a man standing watching me – a civilian who was to become my first husband, and I went on to a life far worse than any war had been for me.

The day peace broke out was the day the war started for me in my personal life. After returning to my home town and feeling so out of place, I married on the rebound and, although my war effort for my country was over, together with my girlish illusions, I then forgot how to giggle for some years. The days of the war had been unkind, in some respects, for so many, but how I often longed to be back amongst all those friends and working together with one common enemy and under one flag of unity.

Thousands of service personnel overseas were anxious to return to their homes; however, a great number had found new loves while they were away.

Alan McDonald served in the army at Canadian Military Headquarters in London, working in records, and came in contact with a lot of servicemen who didn't want to go back to Canada, or at least wanted to postpone their return:

Far more than just some married Canadian servicemen were living with other women in England. I remember one night at an officers' mess at Beachy Head there were about 200 staff and officers in for instruction. I didn't have a girlfriend up town but everybody else did, because in the whole camp all we could get were three guys out to fight this fire in the kitchen in the middle of the night. Everybody else, including the colonel, was living up town.

Some English women had had children with these Canadian servicemen. There were a lot of guys who came back from prisoner-of-war camps who'd been there three and four years and there was some great embarrassment and a lot of fellows had to accept it. A lot of marriages broke up. A lot of women got divorced and came to Canada as war brides.

Take, for example, a guy who was married in Canada and already had two children and didn't want to go home. Now, the army had kind of a responsibility to the citizens and the family back home to straighten him out. It was more a persuasion than anything else. The padres got into it and the commanding officers and there were many complications but I bet most of the guys ended up at home. The personal break-ups when they left England were very difficult.

Even on my own ship, when I finally did come home in 1946, we had guys jump ship within minutes of it pulling out of the harbour. There were things at home that weren't too good. They had parents that had fights. A lot of these fellows never had jobs before, they were out of the Depression. There was a lot of uneasiness at home.

'Coming home' for many was something to be postponed for as long as possible. There were a number of reasons.

Many young Canadians 'grew up' in uniform. In particular, those who left Canada were a very different group from those who hadn't. The stay-at-homes at least had stayed within a train ride of family.

Reports from home were not encouraging. Tooling down from war production put thousands of factories on short staff. The machinery was worn out – tooling up for civilian goods took time and money. Whatever jobs came up, there were hordes of freshly demobilised men and women available. The longer the men were kept in England, the harder it would be to find employment later.

With some exceptions, those who served had no experience in the real world. While being in uniform was not the most comfortable existence, one was fed, clothed, housed and paid. Cancellation of this security made many apprehensive.

Landing in bomb-ravaged Liverpool, Southampton and London

had a sobering effect. The boys who left home quickly became men. Also came freedom. Removed from parental authority and school discipline, with no wife, father, teacher or supervisor to report to, there was a euphoria of being suddenly thrust into self-reliance.

Liaisons with English women were inevitable, with all ranks participating. Of little concern was the possibility that there were already a wife in Canada and/or a husband in Italy – worry about that later. Remember, the Pill had yet to be invented. Needless to say, there were many embarrassments to follow. In the interval – and who knew whether it would be months or years – there were dances and movies and the marvellous pubs before the slow stroll to Victoria Station. In the blackout. Very romantic. What the hell – within a week he could be bombing Germany, dropping in Normandy or reinforcing the Seaforths in Italy.

Those to benefit most from these opportunities were again the 'staff', those semi-permanently on station and having the freedom to 'settle down' in the adjoining town. Some of these arrangements could last for years. Disentanglement threatened to be messy. Many put it off, finding any excuse to avoid the draft home. Their home towns may not be that fondly remembered. These were mature men of the world, at twenty-one. The old song would be repeated: 'How do you keep 'em down on the farm after they've seen Paree?'

There were others who were reluctant to leave Europe. The war had, in Dickens's words, been the best of times and the worst of times. They felt committed to marry the girl and take her home, or at least promise to send for her.

Last, but by no means least, among the reasons for not cheering on VE Day, was the prospect of the return voyage. Nothing matches a troop ship for pure hell on earth. The *Queen Mary* could outrun any German submarine, as could all of the lesser liners. Foul weather was also a good defence. No thought was wasted on the thousands below deck and, indeed, below the waterline.

The captain was happiest in forty-foot waves and completely unconcerned at the waves of vomit that overflowed every toilet, urinal, bath tub and scupper. There may be readers who have experienced seasickness for a few hours and suffered its debilitation. Try it for five days. Having endured such an experience on the way over and convinced it was about to be repeated westbound, the bravest of souls trembled.

For one or several reasons then, at the end of the war, not all were ready to start the third phase of their lives. Some returned to Germany as occupiers, some took their discharge in England, some deserted, some jumped the train between Halifax and home. These were exceptions. Nevertheless, very many of those who did what was expected of them – who were faithful, unfaithful or some-where between – and who returned home had some fears of the post-war years – some founded, some unfounded – but, from the perspective viewed from overseas, they were very real.

'Coming home' was not merely a trip, it was a major adjustment, fully understood only by those who had to make it.

Casey Jackson was in the Forty-Eighth Highlanders:

The war was over. We were in The Hague and, as a country boy from the backwoods, I was really enjoying the free and easy life there after the fighting. Lots of booze (some kinds that I had never heard of but, oh, so good). Lots of beautiful girls.

Drafts were going back to Canada and, as I was one of the senior members in point of service, I had several chances to go back. Since the nightlife there was so enjoyable I turned down the chance. Of course, I didn't tell my parents about this.

However, my mother wrote to her Member of Parliament and said, in effect, 'Herbie Armstrong was only overseas for three years and he is home, but my son has been there for well over five years and he is still there.'

Margaret Spencer was married in 1942, when her fiancé was on seven days' leave. Her husband was demobbed in late 1945:

We were on top of the world that great day. I don't remember too much of our celebrating the occasion in our local pub, but dimly recall ending up in a strange house among convivial but total strangers, all toasting the new era!

Our first priority was to make application to the MOD for possession of a modest little house out of London we had started to buy before the end of the war. In seventh heaven we moved into a much dilapidated property, overrun with mice and precious little in worldly goods. It was Buckingham Palace to us and, with bits and pieces donated by kindly relatives and second-hand shops, bare floor and staircase, we proudly set up home. (An orange box and old card table did kitchen duty for many months!) Our few items were transported by an old horse-drawn removal van (petrol not permitting) and we 'camped out' under these circumstances for a year or so. New goods were a long time filtering into the shops and were of very inferior quality at an exorbitant price few of us could afford. The only immediate post-war items obtainable for newly-weds were government-controlled utility issue. These comprised a bed, wardrobe and chest, *one* fireside chair, two blankets and *three* sheets! The items of furniture were available in two choices of wood and, as all prices were government controlled, I chose a top London store to supply us in order to gain maximum snob value from its delivery van. (Some of us being more equal than others, eh?!)

Despite this humble start, we settled into a happy marriage – my husband soon adjusted to new, permanent, local employment. I left city life and, in the severe winter of '47, we contributed to that year's post-war baby boom. Austerity was still the keynote of those early years. Expectant mums received supplementary free milk, cod liver oil and orange juice, and baby clothes were limited to coupon rationing. Babies also received the same supplementary rations and were reared on a formidable formula of National Dried Milk in huge blue and silver tins, and all seemed to thrive and grow into healthy adults. I pushed my offspring around in a utility pram resembling a small invasion landing-craft on four small wheels, which had to do double duty for fetching coke from our local depot during the '47 winter, minus, of course, the 'pride and joy' left at home in the warm!

For Jean Long, the memories of the end of the war are very mixed:

After the parties, celebrations and parades life became (for me) dull and uninteresting. Strange as it sounds, I missed the sirens, the whine of bombs. The togetherness of neighbours and friends had somehow disappeared. We still had a few foreign servicemen, but the city had gone quiet, only the bombed-out shell remained. Food became scarce, especially fresh fruit and vegetables.

The first Christmas was very austere. We were still getting rationed goods but there were no decent fruits. Our Christmas tree was a piece of holly dressed up with home-made baubles, but the gleaming red berries brightened it up a lot. It was very cold. I remember wrapping up my two children warmly and taking them in the pram to get wood for the fire. It was so frosty that the grass crackled under foot and hands stuck to the wood we were gathering along the lane. Meals were still very difficult to think up. I tried to give them at least one hot meal a day.

My husband did not return home until November 1946. I had brought up my two children on my own. The youngest, a son, did not see his father until he was four years old. They couldn't get on at all. It all ended up in my son being beaten. I can't really blame my husband. It was the war. We had been apart for four years. In those days soldiers did not get leave every few months.

In the end we divorced. He left me with three children. He couldn't get work and, after being in the army for six years, he found home life difficult and boring. My independence had gone, so had my husband. So, like the city I loved, I had to pick up the pieces and try to get on with my life. I had lost my home during the Blitz; I couldn't afford to replace it anyway. Gone was my home, my job, my husband. I think it's called 'war experiences'.

I am now seventy-two, but my memories are still very vivid, very real. But I am not bitter. I feel some of my happiest days were during the war, when I lived day by day.

For Yvonne Garry, Christmas of 1945 was a strange celebration:

One scarcely knew how to approach the season. On the one hand it was a time to be thankful that the recent bloody conflict was behind us and, on the other, well, there were still the shortages and rationing of food challenging the ingenuity of the British housewife. World War II had not had time to fade from our memories and we were still instinctively ducking at the throb of aeroplane engines, even though the skies no longer held a threat.

My family had been lucky. We emerged from the war relatively unscathed. There had been partings, yes, and since home was in south-east London, our house had sustained considerable bombing damage. However, the festive season found we three – Mother, Dad and myself, the pre-teen daughter – once more together under one roof.

My ever-resourceful mother had managed to acquire a turkey and other traditional goodies, the origins of which we knew better than to pursue. Christmas morning was redolent with the mouth-watering aromas of roasting fowl, sage and onion stuffing, and an ersatz plum pudding steaming away merrily on the stove. While we waited for the meal to be cooked, the three of us huddled around a small fire in the front-room parlour and exchanged simple gifts.

Dad got up and went over the window to check on the weather and, as he twitched aside the lace curtains, he noticed two bedraggled-looking pedestrians making their way along the otherwise deserted street. Hands trust in the pockets of shapeless jackets, shoulders and capped heads hunched down against the bitter wind as they passed his view, my father saw the large letters POW emblazoned on their backs. He called us over to the window to watch them trudge up our hilly road.

'Poor blighters!' Dad remarked. 'Won't be much of a Christmas for them.'

My mother's initial reaction to this observation was less charitable. Something to the effect that twice in her lifetime the Germans had caused misery and she wasn't about to waste sympathy on them now. But, as I knew it would, her bitterness lasted only a few seconds. The sight of those grey-clad, dejected figures, combined with the sense of thanksgiving and expansiveness of the season, brought her better self to the fore.

With a sudden shove at me, she urged, 'Run after them, Yvonne! Quick now! Tell them to come and share Christmas dinner with us.'

Without stopping to put on a coat, I fled up the street as fast as my twelve-year-old legs could run and somehow managed to make my mission understood. A couple of minutes later I returned with the enemy rounded up and in tow. They were young men we judged to be in their mid-twenties, and their names were Heinz and Fritz. This much was all they were willing to tell us, even though my father could speak a little German and tried his best to assure them of our good intentions.

It was a strange Christmas meal we five shared. The dinner was appreciated, I think, and yet I remember our guests looking apprehensively at their loaded plates and seeming, at first, reluctant to tuck in.

'Good God, Gwen, surely they don't think we're trying to poison them,' Dad said, half-jokingly.

Mother came to the rescue by producing yet another gastronomic miracle – a bottle of liqueur. Drinks were poured for us all, Heinz and Fritz watching us carefully as we raised our glasses in a toast to the end of enmity. Since the host, hostess and child did not show any ill effects from this libation, the two young soldiers allowed themselves to follow suit and the first small gesture of trust and healing was made.

After the meal we invited them to share the warmth of the parlour hearth and a carol singsong around our piano. The invitation was declined with formal bows and heel clicks. It was really still too early in the aftermath of war for the two nationalities to be comfortable with each other. We watched them resume their lonely plodding en route back to the POW camp. It had been a strangely unsatisfying experience and yet a step we could not stop ourselves from taking. Almost a half-century later, if they are still alive, I wonder whether Heinz and Fritz recall that first bleak Christmas Day before their repatriation and the impulsive hospitality of a British family?

Epilogue

*I*T HAD NOT *been easy looking to the future when the present was so uncertain. Listening to the bombers overhead, struggling to control a plane that had been hit, worrying where the next torpedo was going to strike left little time to plan for tomorrow. Now families who had survived the years of separation looked forward to a time of well-deserved happiness.*

Unfortunately, for many it was not to be. Men scarred mentally or physically by their experiences faced children who had never seen their fathers. Women who had learned to run their own lives were unwilling to revert to the subservient role that was expected of them. Children found the pattern of their lives disrupted by a stranger called Daddy.

The casualties of war were not restricted to those on active service or the victims of the Blitz. There was a tenfold increase in divorces, reaching a peak of 60,000 in Britain in 1947. Servicemen tried unsuccessfully to find jobs with decent wages to compensate for the lost years. Rationing lingered on and even some whose homes had survived were forced to leave them through shortage of money.

Much has been made of the soldiers who went off to war, to serve their country and fight for freedom. Yet behind these men was a hidden army of women who had also learned to fight for freedom. Freedom to be themselves. Freedom to go where they pleased without exciting criticism or ridicule. Freedom to enjoy a life that gave them independence and the power to control their own destiny. It was acknowledged that they had played a major part in the victory. All that remained was for them to have an equal part of the rewards.

The land fit for heroes — and heroines — to live in was once more a dream that failed to become reality. After six years of war, many found it almost as hard to survive the peace.